YOUR BODY IS A GIFT

Mimmy Loftin

**An FYI Guide Book on
Relationship, Love & Sexuality
for Tween and Teen Girls
& Brave Parents**

Listen

CONTENTS

PART 3—YOU BEAUTIFUL YOU

FORWARD

I can count on a single hand the number of times someone's work has made an immediate impact on me. I remember the day I ran into Mimmy Loftin, I had just completed a book to help young women recover from an eating disorder and perfectionism. Both of our topics are taboo. But she was not afraid.

"I just finished a book to help tween and teen girls and their parents talk about love, relationship and sexuality. My inner teenager came out. I was terrified. I'm 31. And that's the thing. She briefly shared on some of the subject matter; how pornography and certain things shown in media have tricked young girls, young women, and even parents. I squirmed throughout the entire conversation. That's when I knew she was on to something big. She was the aunt I wish I'd had growing up, the one who would share solid information and explain my inner guidance system. I needed someone to combat the messages I was bombarded with from the rest of the world. All I had heard from my parents was "Don't have it and wait." This left a total gap -the reality of what I saw happening with my friends. I felt clueless and confused through high school and college. And I didn't learn what I needed to just because I became sexually active.

This book takes you behind the smoke and mirrors, beyond the vague sex ed classes taught by teachers who must walk a political and legal line leaving teens and millennials, without a clue as to how to think, process and protect ourselves. **YBG** gives girls and parents the history they both need to put what we are seeing today into context. The world has changed A LOT, even since I was a teenager, and I barely left that status 12 years ago. Girls must have real information and a way to find their values and boundaries. The media and advertising machine continue to sell S-E-X at the expense of teens, young women, and today's young males.

Mimmy is the perfect person to have written this book. Her foundation is not from guilt or shame nor is all free and easy. She knew a world that valued love making vs 'having sex". She hates that girls are missing the fun of developing real relationships through real communication. Her **5 Biggies** totally cover this and their importance during teen years. She expects guys to respect girls, requires phone conversations-slams frequent texting, What!!? I GASPED! How would we exist without frequent text messaging? I know, right? From the moment I got a cellphone in my hand my Senior year in high school, (a late adapter, I know, but stick with me!) boys took this shortcut all the time. I hated it. These shortcuts exist in so many ways, online and off, and too often include way too convenient access to hooking up. (Tinder, anyone?!) Because she is back in the dating pool after a long-term marriage, her awareness is acute for what teens are not experiencing (like fun from REAL stuff). She is able to share *dos and don'ts* that are spot on, even (and especially) the parts that make you uncomfortable! The way she connects early sexual activity with self- worth and self- esteem and how to find one's values and boundaries, I loved.

Whether you're a tween or teen (I really feel for you, I do), or a parent trying to figure out what and how to share with your daughter, **YBG** is an incredible resource. Her Story Tales and Cautionary Tales I wish I had read as a teen. Her historical account of birth control, the first sexual revolution, and the media will give you a lot of clarity. If you're a single parent I can see it being very useful in your own life. I like that she gives space for dialogue and journal questions to help a teen connect with each chapter's heavy, but priceless content. **YBG** sheds a lot of light and offers life skill tools I will use for life. Its content shows both parent and adolescent how to define what feels good in their hearts, their heads, and their bodies. Finally, an honorable and

deeper perspective has finally been produced in the 21st century on the how, what and whys concerning love, sexuality and real relationship for today's young girls and caring adults.

Megan Reilly
Author of
Escaping Perfectionism

Dedicated to my mother
Nowlan Carter Crowther

Teacher, Mother of 4, Grandmother of 10
& the repeater from Repeats Ville
I Love you and appreciate every little thing
you did for us.

PREFACE

Your heart knows what is true. But this natural knowledge is buried from too much wrong information in today's media. It has confused the best of us. Deep down you know what is right and good for you. Because of all the change in the world, a healthy perspective and relevant information are missing My hope is that YBG brings what you know deep down…into the light. You deserve important information many adults just do not know how or are unwilling to share.

Your emotional intelligence is what will grow as you read each chapter. This requires information, insight and tools. Adults and adolescents will both learn if time & the desire to know is present. Having the right information builds insight and helps you trust yourself. As you read, you may find yourself thinking, 'I know that.' Great! And what you learn or find interesting? Simply underline that part or place a star next to it.

Discernment: the ability to perceive a situation, person or thing with an objective outlook and conclude its placement and/or relevance to one's values and standards of being.

At the heart of emotional intelligence is the ability to discern. You will need to do this while reading YBG. Discernment is not judgement. Discernment is a form of wisdom that helps keep us safe. For only when one learns to discern, will guilt and shame fall off the grid and allow your awesome heart and spirit to kick in and guide you.

Journals rock and can settle your most confusing thoughts & feelings

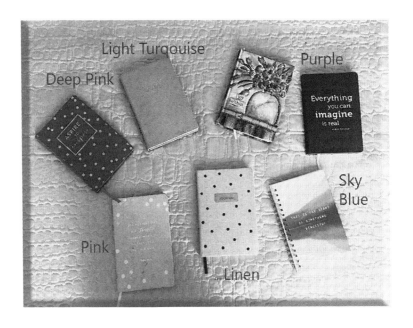

HOW TO USE THIS BOOK

Please Read the Introduction and Chapter 1. If you have a willing Mom, Dad, stepparent, or an adult you trust, and respect ask her to read the chapter. Now the two of you come together.

(This is not a requirement. Just a suggestion. You having information is first and foremost)

Sit somewhere cozy. Perhaps you at the end of their bed—where you can both curl up comfortably.

Maybe flip a coin on who goes first . . . to share about the chapter you both have read. ☺

What are your thoughts? What did you agree or not agree with and why? Just share. There is no right or wrong. If there is a **Dialogue Q & A** section in the chapter, flip to it and share your answers. You will be doing this by yourself in a journal.

Journal-wise – Please purchase one. Very cool ones at TJ Maxx or Home Goods. You are welcome to keep your writing private or, if you feel safe and supported, tell Mom or trusted adult, "Hey . . . I want to read you what I wrote on the Journal Questions." If they listen . . . great. But note that *a lot of parents* may not be up to this. Their loss.

Important

Nothing is set in stone. If mom or dad are not able . . . that's OK. Do what's comfortable, and even a little uncomfortable for you. Just be brave and read <u>YBG</u> and journal on your own. *After all, this manuscript is for you.*

*Confidence happens with information.
*Confidence happens when making a decision.
*Confidence is taking action.

Take heart in knowing you now have a path; a way to grow from the inside where self-confidence and self-respect are created.

I N T R O D U C T I O N

You are a female. This is a big deal. It is vital that you learn why and how to make decisions that protect the best and most scared parts of you. As a teen you are fully capable of learning some things about life and applying logic. And adolescence is the perfect time for this.

I wrote this book because I'm tired of watching young girls get tricked; even so-called *good girls and young women today are* getting tricked. Girls today have almost zero information on real communication, relationships, love, and sexuality. Sex education has failed to offer young females' information that will help you stay on the "right path" for you. Today's hyper-sexualized society has created this mess. No one is telling the truth about sexuality and its connection to love, relationship and trust, and most importantly, to your heart and unique spirit. Today's media is skewed on what a female needs and likes and what guys really like.

*The information you'll discover in this book will grow your self confidence and think before you act (because now you know things) which creates wisdom! Yippee. ***

Most young persons are missing the full experience of real communication and *real* relationships. Simple feelings of love and romance, which are the bomb, get thrown away because of "hooking up" Give us all a break! **Your thoughts and feelings** are deeply connected to your heart. This fact begs to be honored. Emotions and physical touch are meaningful to you in ways that males can forgo. Nature planned it this way. *There's just one problem*—OK . . . maybe more than one: media caters mainly to males. This is one of many reasons it took six years to write this; it contains some heavy chapters.

YBG will give you some hidden truths and Life Skill tools that you will use for life. You will also learn to record in a cool journal ... (TJ Maxx has great ones) your ideas and beliefs. As you read and start to answer the questions in upcoming chapters, you will begin to *feel your own inner knower* slowly grow inside you. This amazing feeling is one of comfort and confidence which, by the way, is where authentic self-confidence happens.

MY BIGGEST HOPE

My BIGGEST hope is that with this book you connect the dots and "get it." By "get it," I mean seeing the bigger picture: the vital connection of your **heart and Spirit** (the essence of you) and your sexuality. You will learn about the **Five Biggies**, like real communication (way more fun than texting), your **VBS** (Values, Boundaries and Standards), and what real intimacy is. **Part 1 and Part 2** were created to help you to slowly *understand* the bigger picture.

TOOLS AND JEWELS

Part Three – **You Beautiful You,** shares with you the jewels inside you. It is the most important part, and the one most all sex educators leave out!! You will learn how to acknowledge, honor and polish them. You have a heart (the first brain/ messaging center) and beauty perfectly born into you.

You will be given simple life skill tools to deal with your feelings and confusing situations.

As you become more familiar with these jewels and tools, you will attract the right situations, people and relationships: be it girlfriends, guy friends, or boyfriends, who will help you on your life journey. Having the right tools *creates healthy interactions, minimalizes heartbreak, and keeps you from feeling used and discarded.*

It's crucial to keep in mind: You are not a guy.

Girls think differently.
Girls feel differently.
Girls love differently.
Knowing one's heart and Spirit is not for sissies.

Disclaimer- This you may be wondering.

I cannot share or teach what I do not know. If I began to speak about same sex intimacy I would be a fool! I have had 2 women friends who came out after ages 30 and age 40. I also had a beautiful big sister, (spiritually speaking) who was in a long-term relationship with a famous female designer. She was the big sister I never had. She had been married and had one son. She claimed her sexuality at 40 something. She died of Cancer 3 years ago or I would probably have interviewed her. But this does not give me *a right or the knowledge* to advise girls who know they like girls. *Guess we will have to wait for another brave soul to write that book. But whoever we fall for ... females love – to be loved when our hearts are open. I do know this. All girls can learn from this book, especially* **Part 3.** Now, let us begin the journey of receiving important truths and *you knowing you* better. This way communication...

> relationships,
>> trust,
>>> romance,
>>>> love &
>>>>> guys
>>>>>> are much easier to enjoy!

Thanks for taking the time!
I promise you won't regret it!
Your new Great Aunt ☺Mimmy

Your "girl" energy is part of your one of-a-kind Spirit, and your greatest guide in helping you value and protect important human connections.

C H A P T E R 1

FEMALE CITY &
THE BIGGER PICTURE

*Nothing is as it seems. There is always a
bigger picture, a greater Truth.*

A STORY TALE - Only Time Will Tell

Once upon a time young girl in high school was able to listen
to a song without thinking about s-e-x. There was a section of
music labeled melodic light rock that often rocked her world.
A song whose lyrics were, "No, you don't know me well . . .
only time will tell . . ." La la la. A sweet wonderful male voice
then sang, "I want to make it with you."

The song was full of love and passion and yet she wasn't
thinking s-e x. Did she ever? Not really. Love, yes. Crush
city? You bet. Undertones of sexuality, for sure, but nothing
blatant. It was love, romance, more love . . . more romance.
Would physical intimacy happen? Only time would tell. Yes,
time, real communication and relationship would have to
develop . . .and she knew to wait; meaning there would be
no heavy physical interaction. But no worries, until then she
could enjoy that song and many others: songs that grabbed

her soul and filled her with feelings of love and care . . . without having to feel the pressure of what girls a few decades later would experience. Yes, "Only time would tell." What fun and freedom there is in simply having a crush, maybe lots of them. Real communication, real relationship and a sense of trust would have to develop first.

THE END

You deserve valuable information about real communication, relationships, romance, love, sexuality, and guys. Unfortunately, important facts and CSGs (Common-Sense Generalizations) have gone into hiding. What has taken their place in our modern world is something almost beyond words. What you are exposed to daily is doing its best to damage one of the most beautiful and natural parts of life: real communication, love, and the ability to have a real relationship. Armed with some facts, insights, and tools, you can learn to do what is best for you as a growing tween and teen girl.

Please keep a journal to be used specifically for YBG. Write down the page number of the book the questions are on. Do your best to answer questions with your heart open, your mind willing, and your Spirit loving. You may or may not want to discuss some of the questions with a trusted adult. It's your call.

WHAT IS WHAT THESE DAYS?

Sex is . . . sex, and love is . . . love. And then there's the in-between. But let's start with the basics. A relationship, romance, love and s-e-x are supposed to go together, naturally. Getting to know someone and beginning to fall for someone is a special kind of dance. It's a process. Love and intimacy

2

are natural gifts to be experienced in their right and perfect time. So how did something so important become twisted to make money and use people?

Becoming knowledgeable about this recent cultural shift will save you unnecessary heartbreak and regret, grow your self-confidence, and increase real love—first for yourself and then for people who deserve your love. Once you receive the information in this book, you will have the basics down.

> You will have a healthy perspective on love and sexuality. You will be able to identify what you value, and your Boundaries. You will know how to act in ways that help you love yourself first, no matter what.

1. You will have a healthy perspective on love and sexuality.
2. You will be able to identify what you value, and your Boundaries.
3. You will know how to act in ways that help you love yourself first, no matter what.

The above will give you an inner confidence, and the ability to guide all the young males you meet on how to respect you, communicate with you and, one day perhaps, love you. But it starts with you.

WHO AM I?

Before we go any further, please think of me as your cool aunt. You know, the one who is kind of "out there" and maybe shares with you a little more than your parents are comfortable with - but they are glad you have the info. Allow me to be your practical and enlightened source of wisdom on the truth about relationships, love, sexual intimacy and guys.

I was a sex educator for many years, and the cofounder of a teen pregnancy coalition in a state that did not allow sex education. I helped create sex-education classes held in a Protestant church. I raised two boys at the time when cable TV and home computers were coming into our living rooms and bedrooms. I had many boyfriends before I married. And after my long-term monogamous (meaning faithful) marriage (22 years) ended, I re-entered the dating scene (tech city) in the 21ˢᵗ century. I know how guys think; young and not so young, I know what they like. But the basics on love, sex and guys, I was taught by my mother as a tween and teen. These basics *still hold true* in today's world and they are . . . priceless! Important laws of nature concerning communication, relationship, trust, romance, love and physical intimacy have not changed. Perhaps this Story Tale will give you some insight.

A STORY TALE

Mom, Me & Boys

Once upon a time, there was a young teen raised by a mother with a keen sense of logic. The girl's mother was also the repeater from Repeats Ville. The mother shared with her daughter, from age eleven on, great lessons about guys, romance, love and sexuality. Having been a cheerleader, the mother shared fun and real-life stories about her own past, while giving her young daughter important information about the facts of life, and guys. The mom's wisdom and practical advice proved priceless in guiding her daughter's active social life and future love life.

As a tween, the girl loved junior high (now called middle school) located in crazy-but-cool Northern California. She

4

loved each day she went to school. At the end of seventh grade, she and her best friend were voted to be cheerleaders by their classmates. They looked forward to the eighth-grade school dances the following year. It was *the time* to dress up, cut up and observe boys--you know, the ones you just might want as a boyfriend.

In the spring of eighth grade, the girls went kind of "boy crazy." Between classes, several of them could be seen holding hands with boys they had crushes on. Then in late spring came the infamous eighth-grade-make-out parties. It was kissing and hugging in the dark, if there was someone you really liked. If not, it was yucko to even think about. I mean, kissing a guy you didn't really like? I don't think so! And why? Because it didn't *feel* okay. This ability to know (and respect) what she felt, kept her from kissing a lot of frogs—I mean guys—unless she really liked one (a guy that is). She knew if she liked him by talking to him, in the hall at school and their long phone calls at night, sharing about whatever they liked.

The process of getting to know a guy often happened through talking on the phone at night. She could hear a boy's attitude, and how he felt, by the *inflection in his voice.* It was a great practice in true communication. It also gave her total freedom at school and at dances to just hang with her friends, dance, practice flirting and enjoy being herself.

Then the following year came the excitement of high school. She and her gang of friends spent the fall and winter getting comfortable. It was new and cool, and so much bigger. She loved observing all the upper classmen, who just seemed much older. She and her buddies from junior high looked forward to the first fall high-school dance. It happened to be a TWIRP Dance. This was where the girl would ask the guy to be her date. It was kind of weird as she knew it was so not cool to chase guys. Her mom's talks reinforced that to chase the guy was to lose the guy. She noticed that if you were popular, you just kind of knew this stuff. And her mom's voice always lingered in her mind. *"They'll drop you like a hot potato."* Or *"Why buy the cow when the milk is free?"* And last but not least, *"Easy is sleazy."* "Okay, okay, I got it!" the girl would often think to herself; reluctantly grateful for the inside information.

The **TWIRP Dance** was the big exception to the unwritten rule of not letting a guy know you liked him. So, the fall of her freshman year she asked a tall sophomore guy on the swim team to the TWIRP Dance. He accepted! Heaven lasted . . . for about a week. In less than ten days she learned that her first high-school crush was just not interested in having a girlfriend. ☺

THE END

I share this true story to give you a quick insight into some basics about how crushes and boys are meant to come and go while you are in school. It's supposed to work this way. Plenty of time is needed to learn, to socialize, accept a seeming rejection, and go on to your next lesson. Many girls today don't know how to simply communicate with guys and how to play at romance. It is more important *today* than ever. Why? Because you are being raised in a fast paced, hyper-sexualized culture and communication today happens mostly by way of technical gadgets.

> I share this true story to give you a quick insight into some basics about how crushes and boys are meant to come and go while you are in school.

The **fun and much-needed practice** of one-on-one communication is not happening naturally in a way that makes you feel good about *you*. Boys today are also missing out - big time. Basic one on one communication skills like calling you and talking on a phone is not happening. This fun 'get to know you and hear your voice' practice is diminishing self-esteem, as he is likely to text you instead of building his sense of self by reaching out and asking you out with a real phone call.

WORDS MATTER

Before we get into one of the most complicated issues on the planet, I must warn you: I have developed a major hang-up about a certain phrase we hear all the time. You can hear it on talk shows, sitcoms, and at school, and even parents today are using it. Things have changed so much and so quickly concerning the disrespect for sexuality, even adults are unaware of what we help create when we blurt out the phrases *"had sex"* and *"having sex."*

Our culture has been remolding us too! I totally stopped saying "had sex" and "having sex" when I realized that even I, Ms. Sex Ed, was disrespecting sexuality just by my casual words. It took a while for me to see that I was degrading relationships and sexual intimacy by blurting out, "had sex" or "having sex." What we say *matters.* Hey, what if we retrained those we love to say, *"They were physically intimate,"* or *"I think they made love,"* or *"They are sexually intimate."* **"Sexual intimacy" is eight syllables and deserves human respect.** Its how babies are created! If you are in a hurry, I guess you could say *"slept with."* Get the picture?

Sexual activity is what creates human life, and the way to begin to truly value intimacy—and up the chances of experiencing romance (without heavy sexual contact)—is by speaking respectfully about physical intimacy. It all begins with how we speak. Honest communication, respect, and love will prove to be a rare commodity if we don't first begin to watch how we talk.

7

Today's media has both trained and tricked us. People didn't used to blurt out about their intimate connections like it was the same thing as turning on a faucet. But the media these days does not want you to think bigger, know a greater truth, or see the bigger picture. This way they can keep us all watching crap and then imitating it. Meanwhile, they rake in big money and lower our standards.

THE FIVE BIGGIES

Please remember when you read (or hear) my smart mouth coming through on a page, that I believe in you, big time. You need not doubt, even when I sound like a mean girl, that you are learning hidden and higher truths about the Five Biggies:

Communication Relationship Trust Romance & Love

Loving and respecting yourself, and knowing how to do this, begins to happen when you get—*really get*—that your heart and your Spirit are connected to love and sexuality. It is the number one goal of this book. Having deeper insight into what's going on in today's world is crucial. Becoming *conscious* can't help but guide you toward doing the right thing, now and later. Hang with me and I will give you the tools to help you become a beautiful soul walking this planet. And you will be able to own it!

LOW ENEGY VIBES

It doesn't take a rocket scientist to see that people are using each other today. I bet you can see and even feel it at school, on TV, in movie theaters and on the internet. Many young girls want to be noticed. Today's mainstream media sells us all out by using sex to sell almost everything. Willing, clueless females are allowing themselves to be used just to get recognition. The most special and private part of a person's life is now often displayed openly *for all to see.* Are you aware that this did not happen *ever* in the history of humankind until twenty years ago? And this has changed everything! Human dignity seems to have fallen into the abyss.

Characteristics like *self-respect and honor—the basis of real love*—are screaming to return. These two values can be hard to find these days. Intimate photos and visuals that once only existed in the pornography industry are out in the world, sadly affecting most of us. For twenty years, pornographic media has slowly become accepted, affecting most of us in ways we have yet to realize.

GENERATION TO DEGENERATION

So how did we in America go from waiting till marriage to "just have sex to have sex?" As a young teen, I asked myself this a lot. I used to love observing societal behavior. American society and sexual behavior changed in my teen years. And I became curious.

So how did we in America go from waiting till marriage to "just have sex to have sex?" As a young teen, I asked myself this a lot.

The last two generations (this includes you) have only seen and experienced what surrounds them. Many young people today think it is "normal" to just go ahead and "have sex." Deep down, though, your heart knows better. And while we are on the subject, "having s-e-x" . . . NEWS FLASH! . . . is anything below the belt. Got that? Girls are fooling themselves to think it isn't.

In Chapter 2, you will discover how the Sexual Revolution of the late 1960s came about, why the youth generation of hippies began to have "lovefests," and why the summer of 1967 was called the Summer of Love. I was super aware of it because I was a freshman in high school and living close to the city known as the city of Free Love: San Francisco. I share this because the operable word in that revolution was ... LOVE. The redeeming quality for most teen girls until the mid to late '90s was that *most* girls understood and honored the important connection and order of the Five Biggies.

Today's full-blown emotional and spiritual disconnect and disrespect of human physical contact—and the intimate act that creates human life, not to mention your heart and Spirit—is still new in our culture. The consequences have yet to be fully acknowledged by society. We are getting closer as the world watches certain American politicians (local, state and national) act despicably, and hearing about the drastic increase in college campus rapes. Both are clear examples of a collective disrespect for females.

WE ARE DIFFERENT

I believe your generation of females will be the difference in bringing humankind back to center. Why? Girls, by nature, have been given something guys have not. We are equal but different. For starters, a female's sex drive is not that of a male's. We are not run by our sexual urges to the degree of intensity that males are. Females are different. We have the ability to apply logic and right action, before or during an intimate encounter. **Yes! You have the ability** to see and feel what is OK and not okay and act upon it. You can also *plan* what to do and

> You have the ability to see and feel what is OK and not okay and act upon it. You can also plan what to do and not do concerning any loving or non-loving situation.

not do concerning any loving or non-loving situation. It's how Mother Nature, God, a Loving Force for Good, the Universe, your loving God of all, planned it! I know this because I have had a lot of practice. And not just in adolescence. But it does take knowledge, self-respect, self-restraint, being conscious and loving yourself. And sometimes you make mistakes. When I was young, magazines that promoted sexual activity for men were called "nudie" magazines. But then something else happened.

When I was in college, *Cosmopolitan* magazine changed its image and content to focus on female sexuality in such a way as to portray us acting like males. And many from my generation bought into it. This magazine was headed by a woman in her 70s. She had missed the Sexual Revolution, *like completely!* What did she know? But more importantly, what did she care about the hypersexuality and future sexual dysfunction that her publication would help create?

Today, magazines, movies and music, the internet, and now the family television are selling your generation of girls (and guys) a lie. Most adults know this, and it's the reason why parents today are freaking out or giving up on sharing with you the bigger picture. Before I go any further, please keep in mind that the media targets *males* 13 to 48 years of age when creating movies, television sitcoms and television ads. But even the guy loses eventually. The marketing world would rather you not know this.

YOU DESERVE THE BIG PICTURE

Let's connect the dots. Did you know that in the US today two out of five girls are sexually assaulted before they get out of college? One third of teen girls experience physical or emotional abuse by a male. And many males use "hookups" to become physical with a girl. By "hookup" I am referring to a boy or young man going online and meeting someone with the specific intention of being sexually active. This is done instead of *taking the time to communicate* one-on-one in person and experience a real relationship. A true relationship requires genuine communication, like asking a girl out and sharing with her. **Most girls and young women** today have not been given a healthy perspective (i.e., the bigger picture) on the psychological and spiritual importance of real relationships, sexual intimacy and love. *This is not your fault.* Most media today have a complete disrespect for all three. Not buying into the media's falsehoods will help save you in all your social interactions, and with guys. A person who is watching TV and movies, or going on the internet, is within eyesight of an onslaught of illicit, violent, and crude visuals that many young guys crave or find humorous, but that have distorted what relationships, romance, love and healthy sexual intimacy really are.

And here's an FYI: What you are seeing (when a creepy visual gets thrown in your face) *is* pornography, not real lovemaking! *Sorry, Mom and Dad. We have to get into this now or we all lose.*

LOVE, THE OPERABLE WORD

So why are so many girls often acting like guys and being aggressive sexually? Do they not understand that they will be tossed aside? An intelligent thirty-something female shared with me, "Mimmy, they don't know what's happening until the fifth or sixth guy blows them off." Not connecting sexual activity with love is directly connected to why many American young men are disrespecting females and getting away with it.

I heard this great rock song recently entitled "Glory of Love." It went, "I am a man who will fight for your honor . . . all in the name of the glory of love." It's a friggin' rock band singing it! It is so powerful that the music and words create feelings of love just by listening to it! It's by Peter Cetera. Check it out.

Listening to songs of love and human connection (rock or slow) was at the core of teen and young-adult life for decades! Cool lifetime memories and *great feelings* bubble up when we hear certain songs still today. These songs will always trigger feelings of love. These are the songs you want to remember. And Nelly's 'Hot in Here' saying its time to take all your clothes off isn't one of them!

Today most teen boys are uncomfortable with all the overt sex talk and girls chasing them. Are you aware of this? A boy's discomfort is directly connected to *the absence of one-on-one communication and a real relationship.* And they have zero help from today's media. I know you are young, but you can get this. And it is crucial you do for the sake of your body, mind, heart, unique Spirit . . . and your future! *Think about the following:*

How do I feel about the subject of love and sex?

1. How do I feel about sexual activity and no love?
2. Am I being fooled, and tricked into believing what the media projects?
3. How can I learn to make informed decisions about my life and be true to my values?
4. What are my values?
5. Am I really supposed to like and want what guys like? (Here's a hint: No)

These are questions you will have the answers to by the end of the book. **The truth is this**: love and sexuality are not easy to discuss. Parents often don't know where to start, especially in today's world. If you have a mom, aunt or willing grandmother, ask her to read the first chapter of the book. You read the same chapter. Now share with each other. Do this only if you respect this relative and trust that she has your best interest at heart. You might feel better reading this book by yourself. Hey, your mom just might be young enough that you both learn something new together!

Identifying your Values, Boundaries, and Standards and the Life Skills Writing Exercises are something you both should do. However, do them on your own and then you can share together. If you are uncomfortable, this is normal. It's OK.

My greatest wish for you is that you *not just read* this book, but that you do the VBS (Values, Boundaries, and Standards) work and the Life Skill writings. You will discover that many of the answers are inside you waiting to be asked, excited for you to grow authentic self-confidence.

> My greatest wish for you is that you not just read this book, but that you do the VBS (Values, Boundaries, and Standards) work and the Life Skill writings. You will discover that many of the answers are inside you waiting to be asked, and you'll start to grow authentic confidence.

Please don't think, "Why don't I know this stuff?" It is normal not to know. What blows me away is having young women in their mid- and late-twenties asking to read this book. When I ask why, almost every one of them has said they'd been given little or no information, and that she had no guidelines! Still, at 25? What's that about? It

14

breaks my heart because *feeling assured of some basics in life* is such a comfort when going through middle school, high school and college.

Here are some basics you will learn:

1. You will be able to identify your Values and Standards.
2. You will establish simple boundaries (physical and emotional) with friends, guys and yourself.
3. You will feel your authentic personal power when practicing discernment and delayed gratification (not as bad as it sounds), as they are social enhancers and health-savers.
4. Having identified your **VBS**, you will begin to honor your feelings and do what is best *for you.*

The above is important because you will have created basic guidelines that will keep you safe, both emotionally and physically. Knowing your VBS frees up your time to have fun, still experience romance and not worry as much. Real freedom comes from beginning to exercise the power of choice when it comes to what you need and don't need to do while still in your teens.

YOUR RESPONSIBILITY

The biggest job you have as a teen is to stay *conscious.* Many girls today are not thinking things through, and are ignoring red flags, because the media has tricked them. I will share something, and risk being called a boy-basher. No way! I love guys. But I want you to become wise and knowledgeable

> The biggest job you have as a teen is to stay conscious. Many girls today are not thinking things through, and are ignoring red flags

about a few things Mom and Dad may be afraid to come out and say, for fear of being politically incorrect or unfair to males. Ha! And just what is correct about pornography going mainstream and becoming today's skewed form of sex education?

CSGs – COMMON SENSE GENERALIZATIONS

You having simple CSGs (simple *must-remembers*) about how guys actually think about sex cannot be emphasized often enough. Just remembering one of these in a time of unknowing can save you from major heartache. So, what is a CSG? Well, common sense speaks for itself. Would you light a match and throw it randomly into dry brush? Generalizations get a bad rap. But they save a lot of teens and adults from doing stupid things. And we are all guilty sometimes of not thinking before we act.

Here are just a few *simple* CSGs to remember. They can help you in all social and romantic situations.

- Females are meant to be in charge of their bodies. What will or will not take place is your responsibility when it comes to physical intimacy. To be clear: YOU call the shots.
- Guys do not like sleazy girls.
- Guys do not like easy girls.

What will or will not take place is your responsibility when it comes to physical intimacy. Guys do not like sleazy girls. Guys do not like easy girls. Guys like the chase: flirting, kissing and one-on-one real communication. Respecting yourself and knowing your Values and Boundaries is a turn-on for a guy.

- Guys like the chase: flirting, kissing and one-on-one real communication. They also love...love, at the "right" time.
- Respecting yourself and knowing your Values and Boundaries is a turn-on for a guy.

AN APOLOGY + STYLE, VALUES & FLIRTING

I am sorry. I am sorry. I am sorry. ☹☹☹ I was told not to apologize. But the truth is, I think most parents today feel bad about what is going on. I have seen many of them completely freak out over the simplest stuff, like seeing their daughter wearing cutoffs (cutoffs that aren't even crazy-sleazy short). Hey, I wore great wine-colored suede ones. They were called hot pants. Picture this! They were hip-huggers, wine suede with snaps on one side and a big cutout turquoise suede butterfly on the hip. But here's the difference. I knew not to wear them to school! Do you? Knowing better is both a Boundary and a Standard. I valued myself enough not to show "it" off at school. I will admit it was hard not to sneak into class just once wearing them with my wine tights, knee-high wine suede boots, and a body suit. ☺

What do you value? You are never too young to learn about *how* and *what* to value. You will be doing this exercise, so listen up. I happen to *value* (besides myself) my freedom! Freedom to be fully me, to dress as I like and to share what is important in my heart. I value one-on-one communication, flirting, affection, romance and love.

I love showing affection, as it is a subtle, beautiful way of showing someone you like

> I love showing affection, as it is a subtle, beautiful way of showing someone you like him, without the complications that come along with sexual intimacy.

17

him, without the complications that come along with sexual intimacy. Are you aware that flirting doesn't mean being overtly sexual? There are plenty of cool aspects of flirting, which you can become quite good at. Flirting is fun and romantic when you know your personal boundaries. Believe me, "having sex" is *so not* the only game in town. In fact, it is not a game at all. Yet people talk and act as if it were. In the Making Out chapter, we'll go into specifics, totally ignoring your parents' greatest fears, by sharing about affection and more.

BECAUSE YOU ARE FEMALE

The consequences of early sexual activity are far greater than we knew back in the '70s, '80s and '90s. The medical community kept most of it under cover until 2005! Moms and Dads often make the mistake of believing that if they talk about sex, in a really honest way, you might make some of their mistakes *or* become sexually active too early. *Actually, just the opposite happens.*

The more you know about sexuality, the less likely you will feel the need to go out and experiment. My own boys were clued in about sexual activity and the technical side by the end of sixth grade. It was cool to see them know the facts. And when I shared (eighteen times! ☺) that sex and love go together, it gave these two boys a higher perspective than what they were beginning to see on television.

OWNING AND FORGIVING

You owning and being in charge of your feelings and body is crucial, as you could be faced with decisions and responsibilities no girl is ready for. A broken heart and feelings of having been used and even abused do not just "go away."

Remember these forever:

- A guy is rarely left with life-altering consequences. A girl is.
- A guy can't get pregnant. You can.
- A guy can go on with his life (like college and another girlfriend).
- A guy can (and often does) leave you to deal with big decisions, decisions that affect the rest of your life.
- You are responsible for a human life for decades. He may not be.

This is the painful reality and the responsibility of being a female.

You knowing your Values, Boundaries, and Standards will help you stay in charge. Say out loud:

I AM IN CHARGE. I AM IN CHARGE. I AM IN CHARGE

Burn it like a big tattoo in your deep inner-knowing place.

Perhaps you or someone you know has engaged in sexual acts in the past. The mistake is felt deep down. Find comfort in the definition of mistake. It is simply a "miss-take" on something that has happened. Even the word "sin" means something very different from what is

A guy is rarely left with life-altering consequences. A girl is. A guy can't get pregnant. You can. A guy can go on with his life (like college and another girlfriend). A guy can (and often does) leave you to deal with big decisions, decisions that affect the rest of your life. You are responsible for a human life for decades. He may not be.

portrayed in many religious communities. A sin is a miss-take. See yourself doing a *re-take*. If you find yourself unable to shake your feelings, there are great writing tools in Chapter 13 to help you. But for right now, try this: **Raise your hands. Spread your fingers open, facing outward. Now, form tight fists. Open up your hands quickly.** *Say out loud with meaning:* "POOF! The past is gone! I am forgiven. Every day is a brand new one." Then look toward your left shoulder and up . . . and smile BIG! ☺

Here are two affirmations you say every day for 21 days. *Look in the mirror and say out loud, twice every day for 21 days:*

I AM A GIFT. MY BODY IS A GIFT.
I AM A GIFT. MY BODY IS A GIFT.
I AM A GIFT. MY BODY IS A GIFT.

And at night before you go to sleep (this is a powerful one!):

I AM IN CHARGE OF MY BODY AND MY THOUGHTS AND I LOVE ME!
NO MATTER WHAT, NO MATTER WHAT!

I hope you are kind of excited about going on this journey to become wise about what love, relationships and sex really are, about how guys think and, most important, about how you are fully capable of creating lasting self-love. You are never too young or too old to learn about real communication, relationship, trust, love, sexual intimacy and your own self-worth. It is never too late to learn what's right for you. But first you need to know what's up (information) and what is in your heart. Only then can you be true to yourself, trust yourself, and act according to your highest and best. My favorite quote for just about everything in life:

"We do better when we know better."

C H A P T E R   2

A BRIEF HISTORY OF SEX PART 1

It is much to your benefit to understand how society evolves or erodes depending on the choices people make.

Since grade school, I have loved observing people and societal behavior. Because I had gone from kindergarten through high school in Arizona, Texas, Washington and California, I became aware that people acted differently in different states. In high school my favorite class (besides art, sewing and drafting) was sociology. My junior year I had this very cool sociology teacher. She pointed out interesting happenings during the time of the Roman Empire and how it fell partly because the rich and powerful were sexually out of control. That always stuck in my mind. So, had Rome lost its values, morals, and standards? Today, in the twenty-first century, we are seeing something very similar.

Knowledge is personal power. As you read this chapter, try and grasp *how and when* American culture began to change. I promise this to be more interesting than studying World War I.

Until the late 1960s, sexual activity outside of marriage was considered unacceptable throughout most of the world. Even today, some Third World countries still see it as a legal, legit reason for stoning women to death. In Europe and America, "houses of ill repute" or "whorehouses" existed for men who chose to pay for sexual gratification. They paid for physical connection. The women were called prostitutes and whores. This is where the word "ho" comes from. These women were not accepted in society, because they sold and traded their bodies for money.

Before the Sexual Revolution, if sexual relations happened outside of marriage, a couple had to be very discreet about it. A woman did not usually share, even with her closest girlfriend, what she might be doing in private with a man. A safe form of birth control was basically nonexistent, and condoms were not always reliable. People often found out that a young woman had been sexually intimate with a man only when she got pregnant. Knowing how not to become pregnant had a great deal to do with a young woman's decision to engage in a private and intimate personal act. Fear of pregnancy, religious beliefs and society's values and standards kept sexual activity private and personal for most people in the world.

> Fear of pregnancy, religious beliefs and society's values and standards kept sexual activity private and personal for most people in the world.

A PENIS GETS A DRESS

Did you know that in the early 1900s condoms were banned in the United States? A brave woman named Margaret Sanger Harris had seen women struggle from having too many children. She herself was one of eleven children. She saw countless women die in childbirth.

In the United States, word spread that French women had ways of greatly decreasing their chances of becoming pregnant. Margaret went to France and discovered they were able to do this with the use of condoms. However, condoms were banned in the United States at the time. This did not stop Margaret! She wanted all women in the US to survive childbirth and have control over how many children they would have. She ignored arbitrary, manmade US laws and put together a plan. While in France, she packed condoms in wine bottles and shipped them to the United States. Thank you, Margaret! This brave soul had all women's best interests at heart. Margaret Sanger Harris was responsible for other firsts that are still considered controversial to this day. And this was back in the 1930s! Look her up on the web. You may find a book or great documentary on her.

In 1916, when Margaret Sanger founded America's first birth control clinic, she and like-minded contemporaries set the foundation for ensuring reproductive rights and access to family planning.

Our grandparents and parents continued this legacy by building a strong national organization, a network of affiliates, and a program for international service.

Perfect...she was not. But Helping women have fewer children and minimizing them dieng from child birth saved more than a mother's life.

THE '50s AND EARLY '60s

Music has always been a great stimulator for love and sexual feelings. However, until the late 1950s, most music and dancing for young and old carried a respectful tone of love and romance. Should a song stir sexual feelings, it was usually subtle and sweet. In music, feeling sexual for a woman was connected to romance. In the 1950s, women had certain steps to follow. Showing off as a sex kitten was not happening, except at burlesque shows and strip clubs. It was romance, romance and more romance. For women, this was great. And though young men rarely needed romance to be physically intimate, they knew to respect a woman, unless she acted and/ or dressed in wildly suggestive ways.

In 1958, a singer from the Deep South showed up on everyone's black-and-white television sets wearing tight black pants. (They would be straight-leg or skinny-leg jeans these days.) His jet-black hair was slicked back, and his eyes sported a mysterious, smoldering look of sexiness. When he sang, he gyrated his hips like no one had ever seen. His deep, sexy voice was undeniable. Whether he was singing a slow song like "Blue Hawaii," or the rock and roll tune "You Aint Nothing but a Hound Dog," young girls and mothers became screaming fans. His music carried with it a sexual energy that came out of the closet and smack dab into the American living room. His name was Elvis Presley, known today as the King of Rock and Roll. Elvis made many fun and romantic movies that young

> When he sang, he gyrated his hips like no one had ever seen. His deep, sexy voice was undeniable. Whether he was singings a slow song like "Blue Hawaii," or the rock and roll tune "You Aint Nothing but a Hound Dog," young girls and mothers became screaming fans.

girls and their mothers could watch together. A new romantic and sexual aspect of pop culture had entered American life. **Elvis Presley** had a beautiful female costar who appeared in many of his movies. She was a cute and sexy redhead named Ann-Margret. She showed American girls how to have fun learning sexy dance moves. She often wore a ruffled crop top and straight tight-legged Capri pants when she danced. She would bend her knees, place her hands on her thighs, throw back her flaming red hair and wiggle like . . . you got it, a sex kitten. Enter sexy dancing for the masses! She and Elvis were cool to watch. Even a ten-year-old who had never heard the word sex could feel something special was happening. It was "sexual energy." This had some parents freaking out.

Along with Elvis came Chubby Checker and James Brown, two amazing black singers the music industry dubbed "Soul Brothers." They both had dance moves every kid over four years old would imitate. These two Soul Brothers danced and moved in ways that made guys and girls get up and move their feet. Oh, my God, what a blast American life had started to become!

THE LATE '60s

The mid- to late-1960s marked the beginning of rock and roll bands. English bands such as The Beatles, the Kinks, and the Rolling Stones began to appear on the music scene, and each band brought its own unique sound. More soul music entered too; amazing groups like The Drifters, The Temptations, and Smokey Robinson and the Miracles. Great girl bands began to appear. The Supremes, The Shirelles, and Martha and the Vandellas brought a soulful, romantic twist and girl-power to teen heart music. Their songs played constantly on the radio and entered the American family living room by way of . . . you got it . . . the television set. Shows like The Ed Sullivan

28

Show knew the whole family would watch when these bands played. Great new music was on radio stations, and American Bandstand and Soul Train were television shows teens looked forward to watching. During this time, too, the United States was dealing with serious world issues.

THE SUMMER OF LOVE

I shared with you in Chapter One that the summer of 1967 will always be historically known as 'The Summer of Love'. This same year, and for several years to follow, the Vietnam War (along with radical protests against it) took over the nightly news. The older generation was troubled. Many young people, college kids especially, protested this war and chilled out to drugs and "Free love." Making love without being married was slowly entering mainstream society. The hippies named making love, "Free love." The famous quote, "Make love, not war," could be seen plastered on walls in the US and in European subway stations. Many older teens, college kids, and young adults in their twenties and thirties began attending hippie music festivals. They were protesting not just the war, but society's conventional rules on how to dress, and the rules around sexual activity.

The Sexual Revolution of the late '60s liberated not just hippies from the conservative life their parents led, but preppy college kids as well. Many young adults were beginning to claim the right to make love, even though they weren't married. However, it was those darn hippy radicals that were blamed for cutting males and females loose from conservative values! Whatever their social standing

> The Sexual Revolution of the late '60s liberated not just hippies from the conservative life their parents led, but preppy college kids as well.

or religious background, young women in their late teens and early twenties thought of sexual intimacy as "making love." You didn't hear people use the term "We had sex" but rather "We made love" or "We slept together." When intercourse happened between two consenting adults or soon-to-be adults the slang term was simply "We did it."

CONNECTING THE DOTS

Connecting sex with love and intimacy was what girls did naturally until the last decade of the twentieth century. To put it another way, their heart was in "it." *"It"* meaning the intimate act of sexual intercourse. The term "getting laid" or "I got some" was used by a guy if he did not really love the girl. Sometimes guys would say, "I used her." And a girl, if she felt safe, might share with a girlfriend that she felt "used" afterwards. **Being in love was important** to almost all women. Making love outside of marriage was not easily accepted by moms and dads, or our culture. To be with a guy sexually and not be in a loving relationship was considered kind of slutty, especially if it happened often. Both girls and guys did not think much of girls who just "did it." Truth be told, a girl who was sexually active and not in a loving relationship was usually left with feelings of having lowered her self-worth. *Because this fact is rarely discussed honestly even today, young females are being hurt.*

Guys are often on a very different playing field where sex is concerned. This is where the word "player" comes from. A male's biological make-up has a lot to do with how and why they think and act as they do sometimes. *It is no different today.* Male hormones are strong, and guys often play the bragging-and-conquest-card if love is not in a physical relationship. This is where the *double standard* shows its colors. It still exists and often leads young women to a downfall of some kind . . . meaning she gets hurt. Yes, her heart (and sense of self) sometimes physically aches.

During the Sexual Revolution, a more effective birth-control pill was developed and became available to women. During this time safe and legal abortions did not exist. There were many horror stories about girls in their late teens and twenties who became child baren becuase of a a 'back alley abortion'. Young women and mothers who were not willing or able to care for a child lived with the fear of potential death from an illegal proceedure. This did not stop women from becoming sexually intimate Or from going where ever they could to end a pregnancy.

The Pill was the beginning of a woman's right to choose. However her physical safety was still in jepordy. Women knew they were risking their life and future should an unwanted pregnancy become her reality. The Pill was a female's best friend should she choose to be sexually active and not be married. Call it perfect timing, or time for change. Change was inevitable. The Seventies were coming and hope and more change were right around the corner.

One of my favorite Journals
-The Summer of LOVE-
summer after freshman year.
Not-The Summer of S - E -X
Don't miss out!

What will never change, despite contraceptive availability, is the biological reality of being a woman. This is why women must be the gatekeepers of any physical encounter (excluding force and coercion). Females are often left with, and carry the burden of, a potential pregnancy and an increased risk of a sexually transmitted disease.

JOURNAL TIME

Please get out your journal. At the top of the page write Chapter 2 Part. 1 pg.____ Please answer each question-*write* them down.

> What will never change, despite contraceptive availability, is the biological reality of being a woman. This is why women must be the gatekeepers of any physical encounter (excluding force and coercion).

1. Can you see yourself liking more than one boy at a time?
2. Why do you think love is important for the female but not always for the guy when involved in a physically intimate act?
3. Why do you think some girls engage in a sexual act and act like it is "no big deal"?

THE '70s

The 1970s was the "Golden Age" of the Sexual Revolution. Though known in history books as a time of sex, drugs and rock and roll, it was a great time to become a young woman. Why? *Picture this in your mind:*

These young women, *around the age of 10* and up had been taught that their body was a gift, that sexual relations were made for love, and that they should *wait.* Young girls looked forward to falling in love. They believed they would wait until then to become sexually intimate. Keep in mind that when these girls were kids, The Pill had not yet been invented. And pregnancy (outside of marriage) was *so* not an option when they were learning about what sexual intimacy was. It was anything but cool to be pregnant, and safe medical procedures to end a pregnancy just did not exist. Back then, in junior high and high school, girls could (and did) easily demand a guy's respect. The standards in society and the media were higher, making it easier for girls to keep their own physical boundaries and standards in check.

Because most young teen girls had their values in place concerning love and sexual activity, girls in junior high (now called middle school) could have fun having a crush on several boys with no thought of having to be sexually intimate. Now, in high school, girls were still enjoying flirting and dating. And yes, many had to check their bases (as in first base, second base, etc.). Girls enjoyed being treated well. Dating rocked and flirting was the bomb. The bottom line: most 14- to 18-year-old girls were able to have fun *without the pressure or complications of heavy sexual activity.*

Guys and girls had the freedom to take their time, create relationships, grow emotionally and discover who they were. Adolescence was *the* time to practice talking, listening on the phone—for that voice inflection- and flirting! Girls often found out what falling in love *felt* like repeatedly-without the intense pressure of having to "*have sex.*" We

Guys and girls had the freedom to take their time, create relationships, grow emotionally and discover who they were. Adolescence was the time to practice talking, listening on the phone—for that voice inflection- and flirting!

often fell hard (as in, a super crush) for several boys. Most girls knew they had to be careful, as no one thought having a child as a teen was cool, and there were no schools to put girls who became pregnant.

Once The Pill become more reliable and available, older teen girls began asking themselves important questions. I was one of them. As a teen, I was fascinated by the change in our culture. I often thought about the many important aspects of becoming sexually intimate. I unknowingly was participating in a practice of consciousness (thinking before acting). I would often ask myself questions like, *doesn't love have something to do with becoming sexually intimate?* And *Hey, this is how babies are made! And now it's like . . . okay?*

As an older teen, I would ask myself the *feeling* question, *'What is okay to do physically with a boy I care about and that would not make me feel bad,* look *bad, or ruin my life?'* This was my practical way of trying to keep my own Values, Boundaries and Standards in place. The saving grace was my mom's advice and honest *shares.* I could see that guys did not like easy chicks. This was fine with me, as I had no desire to be one.

> *When so-called experts say teens don't have the full brain development to make good decisions, don't believe them. Having information and staying conscious allows you to be fully capable.*

The more you want to do what is best for you, the more introspective you become—meaning, the more questions you will ask yourself. Back then, it was pretty simple. There was a real fear of pregnancy and no girl wanted to be known as an "easy lay," feel used, or have a baby.

Q & A –Dialogue Time

1. Do you believe most girls *feel* different today about love and sexuality?
2. Why or why not?
3. Why might it be harder for a girl today to hold on to her values and standards?
4. Do you *know* your personal values?
5. Do you know why *knowing* your physical boundaries matter?

Not all teens in the 70s jumped into the newfound "almost okay" freedom. Many girls had little information on sexual activity. Some girls were simply not responsible, meaning they *forgot* to take The Pill or use a diaphragm. Some girls were then left with the short- and long-term consequences of becoming pregnant. At this time, fearing socially transmitted diseases were not in the "bigger picture" of becoming sexually active. It was all so new. The belief by the general population was that only prostitutes and whores could "get a disease." Ha! How little we knew.

IMPORTANT HISTORICAL NOTE

An important legal and humanitarian event happened in 1973. Up until this time, young girls and women who became pregnant often faced death or near-death experiences from attempting to end a pregnancy. Infections from self-induced abortions and back-alley medical procedures were killing women, young and old. Women had no safe options to end unwanted pregnancies. These unhealthy terminations often left women very sick from severe infection, unable to have children or bleeding to death. Women who felt unable to care for children believed they had no choice in the matter. They often resorted to using objects like coat hangers and knitting needles to abort, taking this often-life-and-death situation into their own hands.

A CAUTIONARY TALE

Senior Year Nightmare

My senior year in high school, a girlfriend of mine found herself pregnant. She shared that she did not know how it had happened the first time. It was in late September, and she flew to Florida to end the pregnancy. When she arrived, she stepped into a taxi. A brown paper bag was put over her head, and she was driven to a hidden spot. The taxi driver had been instructed not to let her see where she was being taken. She said she was terrified and prayed for a safe procedure to end her pregnancy and to return home safely.

The same girlfriend became pregnant again four months later. This time, she flew to New York because the first legal abortion bill had passed in New York. The third time she and her boyfriend went to Mexico. She never shared her repetitive situation with me while we were in high school. I didn't know then she was sexually active. I found out many years later. I asked her, "What did your mother tell you about sex?" "Nothing," was her reply. Three procedures in one year, all with the same boyfriend. What a horrific senior year that had to have been for her. Today, she has four beautiful grown children. She is also left with some scathing memories.

THE END.

During this same time, intelligent, caring women (and some men) pulled together and made the government look at what was happening. Women began to demand the right to a safe and legal medical procedure to end an unwanted pregnancy. In 1973, Roe v. Wade was affirmed by the Supreme Court and passed into law. It was a tough, long-drawn-out battle with religious organizations to have reproductive choice recognized as a woman's right.

During the '70s, American society began to accept that a loving relationship between two consenting young adults would likely become sexual. There was little if any guilt because love and genuine caring were a part of the relationship. Most young women still had their *Values, Boundaries and Standards* that had been created starting around ages 11, 12 and 13. But societal standards were changing from what they had been for centuries.

> During the '70s, American society began to accept that a loving relationship between two consenting young adults would likely become sexual.

What remained in middle America at this time were *basic values* like love and respect for one's self, for your body and for being a female. This had not yet drastically changed. Most young women both desired and demanded respect from their partners. Feeling loved and respected happened for most young women. Regardless of sexual intimacy now being accepted outside of marriage, most females still wanted the ring on their finger and having a baby out of wedlock was not welcomed by either sex.

A safer form of The Pill became available, and the added choice to be sexually intimate was now totally in a woman's hands. The pressure to wait until marriage had greatly lessened. Bigger picture wise – (meaning of major importance in the long run) most women had their values and boundaries intact which kept their self-respect from taking a dive.

Despite the new choice for sexual freedom, young women knew that their sexual behavior *could* affect their relationship with a potential love interest or fiancé. By this I mean a young woman—along with most others of her own age—knew that a young man *might* think less of her depending on her sexual history. (Again, the double standard.) Why was this?

Young women knew something many girls & young women today do not: Guys don't really like easy chicks . . . for very long.

Does this sound politically incorrect? Well it's a **CSG** (Common-Sense Generalization) that still holds true and is *worth remembering.* Being with a respectful guy, and being loved and in a committed, caring relationship, was usually what a girl desired. And it's no different today. Acting like a "ho' was *so* not an option. It was true back then, and girls today, if they are honest, do want respect and love.

> Young women knew something many girls & young women today do not: Guys don't really like easy chicks . . . for very long.

Q & A –DIALOGUE TIME –Please *feel free* to write your answers in your journal

1. So why is love and respect not happening as much these days?
2. How do you feel about being respected by
   a. Girls
   b. Boys

c. A boy you would like to become your boyfriend
d. Classmates you do not know

As the '70s progressed, so did sex, drugs, and rock and roll. Though rock and roll lived on, young women in their mid- and late twenties were tired of partying and being wild and free. Many wanted to settle down. How each of *my friends* did this varied. One girl married her first year out of high school, one girl left town, and two girls married during college. As for me, I followed my parents suggestion: *"Wait two years out of college and work* before walking down that infamous aisle to say, "I do.'" This was great advice and somehow it worked out that way for me

JOURNAL TIME

At the top of the page in your Journal write **Chapter 2. Pt. 1 pg.** ___
Please **feel your answers** as you write and keep in mind— Feelings aren't right or wrong; they're just feelings.

1. Do you think you want to be married one day?
   a. Yes   B. No   C. Not sure
2. Please explain your answer. 2 to 3 sentences
3. Is having a child after marriage for you a Standard, a Value, both or neither?
4. How comfortable would you be to have a baby and not be married?
   A. Totally comfortable
   B. A little uncomfortable
   C. Not sure
   D. No way

5. How would you feel about yourself becoming pregnant and not having a committed partner (committed meaning *married*)?

6. How might your future 11-year-old child feel if he or she did not have a committed father?

7. How is the life of an unmarried female, who has a baby, harder? Please make a list.

8. Please explain if you feel it would not be harder and why.

End of Chapter 2 Part 1

CHAPTER 2

A BRIEF HISTORY OF SEX PART 2

*It took another ten years, the public humiliation of
an American president with a 25-year-old female for
us to admit, "OMG! We are creating a mess."*

Please be patient: This is a section your
mother & you will relate to . . . and **you may
begin to see a bigger picture.** This creates
wisdom.

THE '80s

In the '80s, American society's basic family values were still
in place, but many in our culture started to hyper focus on
making money . . . big money. For many, it was important
to have a prestigious job, create a great income and own a
beautiful home or two. Yes, money, money, and more money.
   What rolled in during the mid-'80s was a 200-foot
media wave. Cable television and VHS cameras and video
players came into the home and changed life as we knew it.
Sexy music and videos, with highly suggestive images, began

to appear by way of something new: MTV. Many of the videos were awesome, even artistic. But the standards that network television always had in place to protect children and young people were not cable TV's concern. Movies that had an R rating could now be seen on cable TV. VHS tapes could also be rented, making it easier for children to get access to adult shows. Most parents were doing their best to see that R-rated movies were not viewed by their kids, but the guidelines to protect the heart and spirit of growing minds were just beginning to be broken.

> What rolled in during the mid-'80s was a 200-foot media wave. Cable television and VHS cameras and video players came into the home and changed life as we knew it.

Before Cable TV, swear words were not allowed on television. But now they were creeping into not just movies, but songs kids and their moms heard on the radio as they drove to school in the morning. Suddenly, Madonna was not just on the radio, but danced on MTV wearing only a bra, girdle and stockings, for all to see.

Cable TV was free of the regulations that the three major networks, NBC, CBS, and ABC—had always adhered to. And then something strange happened. FOX became the fourth national TV network. Their shows started pushing the boundaries of traditional broadcast standards. And they considered themselves the conservative network? Parents of young children began to quietly freak out and feel powerless. It was like their rock-and-roll generation was turning against them. Most *30-something* parents still wanted to hold onto many of the Values and Standards of their parents.

Q & A – Dialogue Time

Here's something you can discuss with Mom or Dad:

1. Ask them if they remember the change in what they saw on TV? If they were in their twenties and not married with children, they may not have noticed.
2. Ask them what their favorite TV show was.
3. Ask what their favorite MTV video was, and why.

In most of the movies in the '80s, love and sexual activity were still connected. Movies like *An Officer and a Gentleman, Top Gun, Wall Street* and a few others actually had plots! The romance scenes were sexy but directed with class and style. Here's my take on it. The post-hippie generation had settled down into marriage, and a semi-nude, sexy and romantic love scene was a great "Saturday Night at the Movies" tease for married couples in their thirties and forties.

But then something unexpected happened in the late 80s. A couple of R-rated movies with underage girls in them came out. They looked funny and fun, but were sexually explicit (highly erotic), and they were *made for adults.* Some older teens were finding these movies. This gave certain young movie makers the *less than bright* idea that even bigger money could be made.

These adult movies laid the ground work for a new category, teen sex comedies. They became popular in the

late 90s. Can you guess what started disappearing? Yep.
<u>Values, boundaries and standards</u>.

AIDS ENTERS THE WORLD

In the '80s, the sexual revolutionaries, middle of the road
and college conservatives were now in their thirties and forties.
Something happened that shook all sexually active persons.
Married and single people were forced to open their eyes
very wide. AIDS (Acquired Immune Deficiency Syndrome),
a new and deadly sexually transmitted disease had entered
the world. The evening news began reporting the number of
young gay men who had died that day of a disease with no
cure. The fashion and design world were losing many talented
artists. At the time, AIDS was still thought to be strictly a
disease homosexual males contracted.

And then came the story of a wife and mother in a
fifteen-year monogamous (meaning faithful, having only one
partner) marriage. She contracted the disease from a blood
transfusion and died three years later. Her death was a major
wake-up call for all sexually active people. Heterosexual male
and female couples realized they too could be at risk. There
was no known cure, and no one knew what to do. Being
monogamous became very important, more so than in the late
'60s or '70s. (On a personal note, I was grateful to be married,
and in a monogamous marriage.) AIDS woke up the formerly
wild, hippie/free-love generation and got us thinking seriously
about our own sexual past. A new question came out of this,
and stirred silently for many years in most sexually active
persons: *Would some of us die from having had sex before
marriage?* No one was laughing about Free Love now. Single
young adults had good reason to be frightened.

Despite the AIDS crisis, MTV and the four major
networks began to push the moral standards of television still

a little lower. FOX (the new guy in town), with its TV sitcom standards lower than NBC, ABC or CBS, continued to baffle parents. *Was this really happening?* Parents at the time wanted to believe it was all a bad joke, that the film and TV industries would somehow clean up their act. Wishful thinking. A few good love stories still managed to find their way into the movie theaters. Love and being in an intimate relationship was still the chosen way to go. No one was dying to be a "ho," date one, or be known as one.

THE '90s

In 1991, jaw-dropping news hit the airwaves: Magic Johnson, the basketball legend who had just married his longtime girlfriend, announced that he had tested positive for the HIV virus, which was known to cause AIDS. But how could this happen to a famous heterosexual, married sports figure? Testing positive for HIV?! It was another huge wake-up call.

There were several turning points in the downward slide of Standards and Values during this decade. Music was the most obvious. Radio was *the* way we heard the top-forty hits of the time. Concerts and MTV videos continued to be amazingly creative, but the values and standards were highly questionable. Visual standards continued to slide lower. The music videos were now showing in almost every family television set that had cable.

Madonna's videos were a prime example. This young woman lost her mother at a very young age. She was raised in the Catholic Church by her father, who was most likely doing his best. Her music was good. It truly was. But her MTV and VH1 videos pushed the standards of decency. She dared anyone to stop her from saying, doing or dressing as she liked. Madonna was determined to turn society on its head. Then she created a visual book, called _The Sex Book_. It was the first time Middle American teens saw women kissing women, right there on a large double-page photo book sold in Barnes & Noble. But in Barnes & Nobles favor, the book was wrapped in clear plastic and could not be opened unless purchased. No, her book was not Playboy or a pornography publication, but the visual creation of an angry young woman to get attention, make money and music. Until then, it had been mainly men who got raunchy in dress and talk. The exception: a female in a pornographic magazine or movie. Pornography existed, but it was by no means mainstream as it is today.

Madonna was like a bridge to pornography. Technically, it was labeled "erotica." But now young women who dared to... could dress sleazily. This was not a style any mother wished her daughters to copy. But they did. Nine and ten-year-old girls began showing up on Halloween, dressed like Madonna. It was creepy. Mothers liked Madonna's music. I was one of them, I have 4 of her CDs; but a role model she was not.

> Nine and ten-year-old girls began showing up on Halloween, dressed like Madonna. It was creepy. Mothers liked Madonna's music. I was one of them, I have 4 of her CDs; but a role model she was not.

Exposed bra straps and underwear in public were slowly becoming part of the teen scene. Showing bra straps had always been considered tasteless and cheap. Standards and values seemed to unofficially cease to exist. If a nine-year-old girl could parade around in public dressed (or undressed) like Madonna . . . in the Bible Belt . . . then anything was possible. America seemed to be heading into an _anything goes, nothing-off-limits_ future. You know what they say about ducks—if it walks like a duck and quacks like one . . . it's probably a duck. But on a 9-year-old? It wasn't cute.

In 1998 the duck quacked super loud when the international sex scandal of President Bill Clinton and Monica Lewinsky first broke. It almost ruined her life, but he survived it just fine, thank you very much. What happened is a *classic example of the double standard* (more about this concept later). The scandal may have redefined what "sex" is (or is not). If you were in middle school or high school at the time, it became one of those *"I remember when . . ."* life events.

For past generations, *remember when* memories had been the assassination of a president or the killing of a famous and beloved peace leader. This is what happens when a society lowers the bar on its Values and Standards. Men think and act differently from women. This international scandal was proof. If you must, go to Chapter 7 to read about this scandal. But if you can . . . wait! I'm in the middle of a history lesson!

By the late '90s, computers and the internet were becoming a staple in most homes. Nobody really knew what they were doing. E-mail was new and promising. But then someone would accidentally click on a site where a naked woman popped up in their face. It was a challenge to be a parent and explain to your child, "Uh . . . sorry, honey, I have no clue why this smut is on our computer!"

I think your parents feel the same way today.

Q & A – DIALOGUE TIME

Ask Mom or Dad:

1. Do you remember when AIDS happened?
2. Were you scared? Why or why not?
3. Where were you living when computers came into American homes?
4. When did you get your first computer?

Isn't it interesting? As I wrap up this six-year project, I'm reading the quote at the top of this chapter about an American president and how we (adults) created a mess. Well, 20 years later. . . it's now a **super mess**. Sexual harassment, sexual assaults and the 'Me Too' movement has resulted in firing professional males from Hollywood to Washington D C. The present president (as of 2018) is... well, let's not go there on paper. But it's also PERFECT timing. Things must get worse before we wise up. It is the nature of the human condition.

I see all generations becoming fully awake because of this mess.

C H A P T E R   3

OUR TWISTED MEDIA

Connecting the Dots
You can't fix what you don't know is broken.

Depending on your age and life experiences, you have a certain personal perspective on life. When given new information, your perspective is meant to expand and evolve. This is what makes a person wise.

You have been born into a world of instant access to the internet, cable TV, movies and television shows that allow sexual content. All four of these today allow human violence and pornography into your visual realm. This fact has slowly distorted human communication, respect, real relationships, love and intimacy. It has also put a major kink in creating a healthy life-perspective.

"Why am I still reading about the media?" may be what you're thinking.

Because it has taken over our lives in almost every way. And it is *so* past time for us all to see life from a higher perspective. This takes information many

And it is so past time for us all to see life from a higher perspective. This takes information many people don't seem to have nowadays.

people don't seem to have nowadays. What most adults know to be true (from back in the day) has gotten lost with all the over stimulation and distortion in media. It is important that you have the information in **Chapters 2 and 3** so you **can see the Bigger Picture**.

With knowledge comes personal power - the power to make good choices.

VIDEO MADNESS

The first weird shift in media actually began, domestically, *before* cable TV. It started when Super 8 and VHS cameras and tape machines came into the home. VHS cameras made shooting a baby's first walk and first words, or an eight-year-old's first dance recital, easily seen on a television set. Most adults saw it as a family-life enhancer. But it also gave some people the less-than-bright idea to shoot sexual content.

A FIRST

In 1986, the first domestic "sex tape" was made by a young Hollywood heartthrob. Until this 20-something teen idol decided to record his sexual activity with an unknowing 15-year-old girl (a moral and legal violation), filming a sexual act was left to the lower realms of humankind: the pornography industry.

The national news reported that this Hollywood teen heartthrob had violated a young girl's trust. It was probably the first time American nightly news had ever reported a sexual violation that was not rape but something else. Most of America felt shocked and disgusted. Teens and adults knew that videotaping a sexual act was below the standards of most thinking and feeling human beings. But this young actor went "unconscious." He did not think it through when he videotaped himself and the unsuspecting, underage girl. He thought it was cool. Great. Welcome to the beginning of pornography going mainstream and shared on the nightly news!

PERSONAL STORY

Two years after the famous Rob Lowe sex tape was hyped up on television and shared with the world, three Texas college fraternity boys were taken to court for filming a young coed without her consent. Remember this was *before* internet and celebrity online sex videos. The American public was disgusted to learn that two of the three young educated males did not have enough respect for sexual engagement than to say to the thoughtless friend who suggested the filming, "Are you nuts?"

I knew the older sister of one of the frat guys. She felt deep shame in sharing it with me. I felt for her. He came from a well-to-do family, and who would have guessed that college boys could be so cruel and thoughtless? In today's world we know that they can be. We even have movies about this behavior, a lot of them. Thanks Hollywood, *Not*.

FLASH FORWARD

Today we have two young "Who's Its," (my title for young women who have done very little) making millions, after having videoed themselves *having sex* and then being given guidance, from parents and outside money-mongers, to capitalize on their unsacred act. Heck, Madonna knew better than to go that far. Then again, she may also have been ticked off that she didn't think of it. Today Paris Hilton and Kim Kardashian are growing financial empires.

You may be young, but you are intuitively intelligent. You know a few things parents may not give you credit for. There are emotional after effects of videotaping sexual behavior that create regret and often haunt those who have done this.

Do yourself a favor. Please turn on your *inner knower* and answer the following questions. You may be young, but you are intuitively intelligent. You know a few things parents may not give you credit for. There are emotional after effects of videotaping sexual behavior that create regret and often haunt those who have done this. Take the time to think and reflect on this. Ask yourself these logical questions. Write down the answers. This practice will help you develop into a conscious and caring human being; a practice many adults have yet to learn.

JOURNAL TIME

Please *think and feel* your answers as you write.

1. Does videotaping the most private human act of intimacy, which at its highest purpose results in creating a human being, feel OK to you?
2. Why would you do or not do this?
3. What might it take for a girl to decide to make a *sex* tape?
4. What must she not *feel* or not care about to make a *sex* video?

5. Were you aware, before you read this book, that videotaping a sex act had always been a pornographic activity?

Your ability to answer these questions is helping you to know your Values and Standards, a practice we will work on in depth in **Part 3 - You Beautiful You.**

It has never been okay for females to make a sex tape (though some do), as it will one day take down their self-respect and self-worth. However, it's not just porn actors in low-rent films showing a rough-and-tough version of a sexual act. Few people want to be portrayed as porn stars. Here's the deal: it's sexual but it's not sexy. Does that make sense? Wouldn't you rather have a guy attracted to your natural beauty, your thoughts and your unique way of *being*? That's the sexy I'm referring to. Nothing is sexier than a female or male who has confidence just walking down the street. A girl that attracts a guy just walking past him in a simple dress or slouchy jeans has something she has developed. This girl knows her **VBS** (Values, Boundaries & Standards). It is important to keep in mind that a boy with all his strong sexual feelings, feels safe just knowing that *you know* your values and boundaries. This alone attracts him to you.

> Wouldn't you rather have a guy attracted to your natural beauty, your thoughts and your unique way of being? That's the sexy I'm referring to.

MOVIES

In the mid-'80s, yes, (we are still *back there* but stay with me. I want you to see how valueless standards start to become okay) two adult movies snuck in that had *teens* in them. Not many people saw them, but it was the beginning of accepting something that really was unacceptable. These two movies were not meant for adolescents to view, but to entertain old men who lacked a healthy sex life. One movie was about spring break. It has never been considered OK in American culture to show a grown man hitting on a teenage girl. To make this movie pass as credible for public viewing, a well-respected actor, Michael Caine, was hired to play the "dirty old man." I believe the moviemakers thought they could slide it into movie theaters, and then make the big money later from video stores renting this "made for adults" movie to whoever chose to rent it.

The late, great film critic Roger Ebert said of this movie when it first came out in 1984: *". . . to make a cynical sitcom out of [a serious situation] is questionable . . . But that's what they've done with* Blame It on Rio. *This movie is clearly intended to appeal to the prurient interests of dirty old men of all ages."* Any media showing adults preying on underage girls lowers societal standards. The movie critic was disheartened, but the movie was out. This was a media turning point, showing where American society was headed. If a major movie director puts it out in the world and uses a famous actor . . . who's to stop him?

In 1987, there was a "teen movie" that blatantly showed a boy using a girl sexually. There was even a great lesson in it, but the lesson was downplayed.

SCENARIO: A teen girl was thoughtless and just wanted to "be loved." The boy used her and bragged to friends. She got pregnant. Though he had said he would help her, he skipped out and did not pay for the abortion or pick her up after the procedure. He was nowhere to be seen.

The last scene in the movie showed her and her best girlfriend working at a burger place. She turned to her friend and said,

"I don't really even care about sex. I want a relationship. I want love."

The movie had goofy teen guys making funny comments throughout the film. The viewers were entertained. But the two girls' very telling message said more than all the guys in this film. The important (life changing) situation and message was washed out. I took notice only after seeing it again. The movie is considered a modern-day teen classic, *Fast Times at Ridgemont High.*

Q & A - DIALOGUE TIME

Why do you think the guys funny and crude comments throughout the movie made it a teen hit?

1. Why do you think the challenging situation the teen girl (and guy) were in was downplayed?
2. Do you think a serious teen movie about pregnancy and what to do could ever be a hit movie?
3. Why or why not.

A TURNING POINT FOR AMERICAN TEENS

By the early '90s, young filmmakers had gotten the idea that money could be made by creating *teen sex-comedies.* These movies began to pop up, lowering teen standards and putting big money into young moviemakers' pockets. Teen sex-comedy movies began promoting the

message that "sex for the sake of sex" was okay . . . and funny.

American Pie, **which came out in 1999,** was a perfect example of how low young-adult movies had gone. Many young males were thrilled. But these movies were devaluing young women. *Romance, respect and love* connected to sexual activity had sunk to the bottom of the list. The very things that make life worth living were slowly fading from the big screen and later, real life. Movies about real love started looking like a pipe dream. Smut was becoming the norm.

American Pie, which came out in 1999, was a perfect example of how low young-adult movies had gone. Many young males were thrilled. But these movies were devaluing young women. Romance, respect and love connected to sexual activity had sunk to the bottom of the list.

After reviewing one of the very first teen sex movies, a female New York movie critic shared with her readers that sex comedies were making money, no matter how sleazy or deviant they were. She wrote that a new trend of teen movies was not only highly sexual and showing adult content but were also displaying an "anti-woman" attitude. Our American movies were helping to lower cultural values and derailing the Women's Movement.

Side note: You will gain personal power if you are informed about women's history and see how we got derailed. Your own grandmother or great aunt may have joined protests to have basic rights: to be treated equally, be paid equally, and be free of sexual harassment in the workplace. Today we are seeing young girls giving up their power and self-respect by using sex as something to get boys to like them and to make money. What the last two generations of girls know about guys, communication, respect and relationship must be re-introduced. Why they are important is at the heart of YBG... and can help you wake up the guys!

In 1999, the same year the teen movie *American Pie* came out, an R-rated adult movie did it again. But this time it became a hit. It was in every theater in the US and won movie awards. They got a major movie actor, Kevin Spacey, to play a dad who became obsessed with a teen girl, a cheerleader no less. It was like Hollywood giving the finger to American parents: *"Hey, come see our new morally low-bar movie. We lowered the bar (again) on your Values & Standards. But maybe your children won't watch it on cable one day. We don't want them to get the wrong idea.".*
Parent: *"Yeah, right. Thanks for putting it out there and winning a few awards so that one day we have another movie we have to explain to (or hide from) our tweens and teens."*
From here on out, valueless movies began hitting the theaters and then entered homes. Healthy censorship went out the window by the year 2000. Computers, now in the home, did not help parents oversee improper content. They enhanced it.
It is worth noting that a movie made in 1999, still as crude as ever, is these days considered a classic. But hear what one 15-year-old surfer in 2016 shared with me about this movie, after his dad had checked it out for him. I asked him if he watched it with his dad. "No way . . ." But his father checked it out for him! *What's that about? It's called 'unconscious parenting'.*

TELEVISION LAND IN TODAY'S WORLD

Here is a scene from a recent television sitcom. It is on one of the four big national television networks, one that used to have high standards. **Set-up:** Jessica has a best male buddy named Jake. Jessica also has a new friend named Lindsey. Jessica has not yet told Jake about her new friend Lindsey. Apparently, Jake met Lindsey on his own in the local coffee shop.

SCENE: Lindsey (Jessica's new friend) walks out of Jake's bedroom with a sheet wrapped around her. It is in the middle of the afternoon. Jessica is sitting in the living room. She quickly blinks her eyes, surprised at what she is seeing. Then Jake walks out of his bedroom behind Lindsey. Jessica sees them both and says, "Hi," embarrassed and totally blown away, she adds, "Oh, I didn't know you two knew each other." Lindsey giggles, somewhat embarrassed, and says, "Uh . . . uh . . . yeah, we met at the coffee shop today."

Too many thoughtless, valueless sitcoms are on primetime television. If you think a young woman sleeping with a guy after meeting him for coffee is respectable and normal human behavior, you would be wrong. However, most of you have been exposed to TV and movies that have been showing this exact kind of behavior, repeatedly. You have likely heard about or participated in online "hookups." Even the best of us are influenced by today's lower standards. You *may think* that most people—smart, respectable, quality human beings—would see nothing wrong or weird with this sit com set up, but you will have *been fooled*. This very scene was put in the sitcom to freak people out. Instead, it confuses, hurts, and lowers the standards of human respect for others.

After reading this sitcom set-up, my brilliant 15-year-old girl editor wrote in red pen-

"They stole our innocence."

JOURNAL TIME

Think it, feel it, write it.

1. What would you be thinking if you were Jessica?
2. How would you feel?
3. Why would you feel this way?
4. What would you have said to Lindsey in private?
5. Do you think you may have friends who are capable of *pulling a Lindsey* on you?

THEY STOLE OUR INNOCENCE

Values and standards are lower today for many reasons. But television like this is how we all get tricked. This sitcom would never have been allowed on TV until very recently. Shows like *Married with Children* that contained adult humor slid into American family rooms in the late 1980s and reruns played throughout the '90s.

Teen girls do not naturally think like young males. The media today ignores this completely. It sells to males. Again, the target market in advertising and many television shows and movies is geared towards males 13 to 48 years old.

Did anybody notice it would help downgrade all sitcoms to a new moral low? Parents did. But money and cable TV won. Knowing how and why people slide into a cultural mudhole is part of the key to fixing things. It is called 'being conscious. Parents were clueless twenty years ago because cable was so new, as was the internet. No one thought it would last or get worse. *But then it did.* **Teen girls do not naturally think** like young males. The media today ignores this completely. It sells to males. Again, the target market in advertising and many television shows and movies is geared towards males 13 to 48 years old? Donny Deutsch, a well-known advertising guru, has shared this several times on television talk shows. Is everyone influenced by the decisions of media moguls who make decisions based on how much money can be made? I believe unless your tech free, you are. What we are all exposed to these days has been twisting the hearts and psyches not just of teens, but also of preschoolers and grade-schoolers. By twisting I mean distorting what trust and real relationships are. This change in our culture is a first in the history of the world. And it affects others around the world.

Whenever you see a quick sexual setup on TV or the internet, what you are seeing is not two people who are making love or even in a relationship. The majority of shows and films today do not show love or intimate caring relationships. Do not allow modern-day media to fool you and lower your standards and your chance to live your life without romance, flirting, sharing and caring in an authentic way.

A MEDIA EXERSIZE

- Make an adult decision. (Sorry, it's grown-up time.)
- Flip the channel.
- Make the choice.

- Power down the computer.
- Turn on great dance music.
- Get up and dance!

Make a decision. It's a choice. This is how confidence happens. <u>Confidence is making a decision and then taking action</u>. It totally builds real confidence. **Do not to let media** hurt your ability to experience repeatedly a life of real communication, relationship, romance, love, and passion. Young people are being reprogrammed to accept smut. *But so are adults.* The results today are everywhere. Girls in school dressing and acting in smutty, slutty ways is a blatant example. And apps for hookups can slam one's self-concept. **Why? How? You ask.**

> Young people are being reprogrammed to accept smut. But so are adults. The results today are everywhere. Girls in school dressing and acting in smutty, slutty ways is a blatant example.

1. *Natural human communication and real relationship development gets squashed.*
2. *One third of young males today are sexually impaired and brain impaired from arrested development of communication skills and the heavy use of pornography...*

> One third of young males today are sexually impaired and brain impaired from arrested development of communication skills and the heavy use of pornography...

You may be thinking, *"But some of the talk shows have women on them and they are always sharing about guys and sex. They talk like sex just to have sex is OK."* Guess what?

If they are under 45 years of age, many of them were in their teens and twenties when sleazebag media began. They were tricked and programmed by teen sex movies, magazines like *Cosmopolitan,* and whatever media could get by with feeding us. And today, even older adults who know better have slacked, sometimes a little, sometimes a lot. We all get influenced.

Here is a perfect example of how the media has played with the values of many (not all) forty-something females: A forty-year-old woman was around 15 or 16 years old when the first teen sex movies and videos began to enter American culture. Today some of these women have talk shows.

TALK SHOW SET-UP –

A beautiful woman (very well dressed) struts around her audience with a microphone in her hand. Her tease question for the almost-all-female audience is:
"Okay, ladies! So, when is it OK to have sex? On the first, second or third date?"

JOURNAL TIME (Open your heart & clear your head)

1. What do you think most women in the audience may be thinking? Or were they?
2. Do you see this question as odd? Why or why not?
3. Why do you think she did not use the term "make love" or "become sexually intimate"?

Many of these women in her audience are mothers today. How does a mom teach a daughter that "making love," being physically intimate, is special and so is her body, that "having sex" is kind of what dogs and guys want first? I won't name the former TV host. She has had relationship issues. But she has a very young daughter. Despite the big money she has made selling products and working on reality TV shows, she knows no better. What will she share with her daughter one day? Perhaps all her miss–takes or mis–perceptions. It will take information and a willingness for her to reflect on her own life. The information and knowledge you are receiving now she does not have. Perhaps she will read this book and gain a healthier perspective and then be able to share with her daughter. Maybe she and her daughter will learn together the importance of healthy relationship interactions.

TV, MOVIES, NETFLIX, AMAZON, ETC.

Our mass media, in all its forms, has consciously and unconsciously programmed people. Even many adults today are talking like it's normal to make *a complete disconnect between sex and love.* Television and movies today rarely portray worthy relationship stories and lessons. It's harder to write those. Sex shows are easy. Writing and showing the sensitivity and specialness of new love—meeting, connecting, flirting and kissing—is not so easy. Maybe that's why *Romeo and Juliet* have been remade so many times.

> Even many adults today are talking like it's normal to make a complete disconnect between sex and love

Hey, why not turn on the computer, open Word and write a short love story yourself? Yes, a sweet, short story that begins with meeting someone. Share how they begin to communicate and develop a friendship and mutual respect. When respect and appreciation is in the air . . . now, play with romance!

The entertainment industry could certainly use a few hundred real relationship scripts, and you could make a bundle! Music, movie and TV executives need to be way more conscious and respectful of children, teens, women and sexuality. Until that day you have the responsibility (respond-ability) to protect your heart, mind and Spirit.

Q & A - DIALOGUE TIME

1. Do you think your generation would like to see programs that show the process of real communication and romance?
2. What recent movies can you name that expand these values and that you feel in your heart are good for you?

So just turn off all the electronic devices? It is doable. Use Mel Robbin's 5, 4, 3, 2, 1 blast off technique to break your habit. (See on YouTube) <u>Mel Robbin's 5 second rule.</u> **This next section tricked me** right after college and it wasn't even electronic. Sadly, what we read is not always in our best interest. Magazines are shiny and colorful, but often carry messages not unlike the *wolf dressed in sheep's clothing.*

MAGAZINES

A CAUTIONARY TALE

Once upon a time, a sweet young woman in her teens moved to the United States from another country. She became sexually active around 21 years old. At age 32, she discovered she had cancer of the cervix. In her sweet accent, she said, "Mimmy, I am so mad. Why would that magazine (Cosmopolitan) say things about having sex with lots of men, if it can give me this disease? I may not be able to have children! What if my operation (a conization) does not take away the spot?"

At the time, she was living with a boyfriend. She had made the decision not to be heavily sexually intimate with him until they married. She was very afraid that this sexually transmitted disease would take away her ability to have a child. She did not have the information that would help her understand that if the medical procedure was successful, she would be okay.

THE END

Another young woman also not raised in the U S shared with me her anger at the same magazine. Both women believed that in the United States everything was better. Neither woman wanted to accept that a magazine for young women would not tell them the *whole truth* about multiple partners and the risks involved. I shared with both young women that I too had been manipulated by this magazine after I left college. And yes, I felt tricked at times. By this I mean that there were times I would think about some article I read, totally biased and written by who knows who. I am living historical proof (ha!) that we do get our clues from the media. As young women, we buy into the sell-sex-at-any-cost articles they write. Back in the day, when "Free love" was first happening, no one knew that "good girls" could get a sexually transmitted disease! Some hard lessons followed many of us years later.

I JUST WISH...

Knowledge and staying aware will help you big time! It bothers me that few grown women to this day share honestly with young girls and young women. I believe it may be due to the fear of being judged. This magazine is still in print and now has a teen version! Go figure. It doesn't matter how many safe-sex articles they write; the full truth is rarely revealed. The greater truth does not generate money. And . . . most media hope you never understand the connection between one's heart and spirit and sexual intimacy. If you did, they would be out of business, but most young women would have today, a higher sense of self-worth.

HEART AND LOVE IN MUSIC

In **Chapter 2**, I went into great detail about how deeply music affects our culture. In the '60s, and through the '90s, music helped shape the way young people dressed and talked. MTV and VH1 teens and young adults were shown how to dress cool. They could simply turn on cable TV. But what were they shown concerning love? Rock bands like the Rolling Stones and the Kinks easily combined their great rock music with love and sex. It was never just a "sex" song. Remember, the radio airwaves had to comply with certain values-and-standards codes, so swear words or overly suggestive music lyrics could not even get on a radio station.

In the '70s, the Eagles were a band whose songs were often about life and misguided ways of love and relationships. Same with bands like Jackson Browne, Bruce Springsteen and America. They were all amazing in choosing words full of passion and love. "Love" being the operable subject matter. And sex? Well, sexual energy could be *felt* in the music. The cool thing was it was *so not* at the top of the list. The music never washed out love and relationship but was the core of a song's lyrics. Teens were able to freely *feel* sexual feelings and *feelings of love* without

> The music never washed out love and relationship but was the core of a song's lyrics. Teens were able to freely feel sexual feelings and feelings of love without the complications of thinking they had to have sex

68

the complications of thinking they had to *have sex*. In other words, girls could breathe, feel the love, and enjoy thinking about a guy just by listening to a song.

In the '80s, it was big-hair bands. Mothers today who were in their teens and 20s back then thought they were sexy. Tight pants, hair sprayed hair and faces with makeup was not uncommon. But no one put them in the category of James Taylor; Crosby, Stills and Nash; and about twenty other '70s bands. The '80s, remember, were about making big money and yet still rocking out to hard rock music with 'love' still in music lyrics. Toward the end of the decade, it was also about "girl music"—Madonna, Cindy Lauper, and the B-52s were the precursors to Lady Gaga, Beyoncé, J-Lo and a few others too raunchy to list. But the list is endless.

Here's the point: Music up until 2000 was *mainly* rock/ heart/love based. Blatant sex was not *always* the main theme. The vibration and the words in the music had sexual overtones but the beat is what compelled people to get up and dance . . . yes, *dance* to the music. Hey, isn't that a song?

The coolest thing about the late '80s and early '90s in media was that every good song had a video and could be seen on a television set! Tom Petty, Michael Jackson, Cindy Lauper; you couldn't help but dance to. Saturday mornings, moms could slip in a fun dance workout between errands and a soccer game. Imitating Beyoncé and J-Lo would not have been cool. Get what I'm saying? I mean, do you really want to see your mom twerk?☺

In the 90s rap music entered the mainstream. It's been around since the 1970s but now it was being fully embraced by the mainstream music scene. It was incredibly vulgar and banned on most radio stations. But big money was made, at the expense of glorifying gangster behavior, gang and gun violence, and violence against women. I know there are a lot of talented artists in the hip hop/rap field. But the vulgar lyrics, the violent lyrics, the objectification and degradation of women—a "bitches and ho's" mentality—has not contributed to a respectful attitude toward women and girls. Hopefully, in the future, rap artists, who today have become role models to young people all over this country and around the world, will put forth a more positive message for their fans to emulate. I believe some are doing this now.

> Have you noticed that great slow songs are not about sex but about l-o-v-e? The heart must be in the song for it to work. A great song conveys a respectful combination. There is a class-and-style element in the way an artist puts the two together.

LOVE IS IN THE AIR

Have you noticed that great slow songs are not about sex but about l-o-v-e? The heart must be in the song for it to work. *A great song conveys a respectful combination.* There is a *class-and-style* element in the way an artist puts the two together. That's a musical artist. When Sade sang, in the early '90s, "Smooth Operator," "No Ordinary Love," and "By Your Side," she beautifully expressed a sexual style with class and ease in a way everyone could listen to and melt over.

One day I asked my 20-year-old editor, "So what do you play if you want to hear romantic music?" Her answer took me aback. It also confirmed something I knew in my heart. She said, "Oh, we just listen to the old songs." Really? But it made sense.

Perhaps Adele does that for some of you. And the guys? Well there's John Mayer, who tells a bit too much about his last girlfriend in his songs (but we forgive him because he is brave and shows his heart). Right? John Legend has a song, "All of Me," so cool and full of love. And then there's Taylor

Swift, who also shares a bit too much. But let's forgive her too. Why? Because she is one of the few visual examples of style and class in the last 15 years. Her style is to be commended. You may love Selena Gomez and Justin Bieber's slow music. Maybe not. I could get into country western, but we would never get to the next chapter!

JOURNAL TIME -Please create three lists in your journal. You will want to look back at these.

Pick any song or movie from any time that creates *feelings* of love.

1. What are your favorite love songs?
2. What are your favorite dance songs?
3. What song(s) make you feel like anything is possible?
4. What are your favorite romance movies?

Please share some songs on Facebook (sorry – but you will need a page) that make you *feel* love is in the air when you listen to them. Go to **Facebook Girls_Your Body is a Gift, or share on the website** www.YourBodyisagift.com

Hope you're ready to get into the 21st century? I sure am.

For centuries **real communication, relationship and love** never had to be spelled out. Untill the late 1990s love and respect were the norm in most music, movies and songs. This *helped guide girls and guys* to know *how and what* to do and say. Now add texting, tweeting and pornographic media and we are all in need of a serious conscious re- training on how to respect human values.

Think Think Think
Use your conscious mind.

She did and today day lives with a
sweet hubby & two little ones.

C H A P T E R   4

SOCIAL MEDIA
& YOUR PHONE

THE POWER OF CHOICE & REAL
COMMUNICATION

WORDS ARE THINGS. What you see, what you say, what you hear can hurt you...for a while or a lifetime. But you're in charge. Take advantage of it.

THE POWER OF CHOICE

Please use a little bit (OK, a lot) of your inner strength and ask yourself, *"Do I Tweet . . . or don't I? Do I Instagram . . . or don't I? Do I use my good energy to slam someone just because . . .?"*

Relationships and real communication have changed because of technology. The worldwide media pretends otherwise. If I had not experienced a Second Adolescence, when texting became 'the thing' I wouldn't understand this stuff well enough to share it with you. But I am finding myself guiding adult males to call instead of text...until we get to know each other better.

"Hey, call me on the P-H-O-N-E big guy.
I want to hear your voice."

Are you leading, or are you being led, by social media? So new is the daily use of electronic gadgets that even many adults wait until their eyes bleed before telling themselves, "This is driving me nuts. I need to get off this energy sucker!" Do you know that you are responsible for deciding *when* to get on an electronic device—i.e., a smart phone, a smart pad, or a computer? *Thinking* before you reach for the phone or computer is just the beginning of a very high brain practice for all human beings who use technology. Have you tied yourself down with decisions to make: Snapchat, texting, Instagram, tweeting, Facebook, e-mail, a music site or website? Is it any wonder *real-life* connections are fading from everyone's life? What if you selected to use just 2 and make life easier? You would cut in half criticism and potential rejection.

Every single time you choose (and it *is* a choice) to *not pick up and turn on* an electronic device, you have made a decision to not risk being thrown left and right emotionally. You probably experience enough emotional ups and downs at school and home without *Electric Gossip City* going on 24/7 on different social media sites. Deciding to answer or not answer your phone is an act of personal power and love. (And I don't mean if you see your mom's number calling that you should ignore it!)

Using your decision-making power is a great practice in growing your sense of self-worth. Why? Because the more choices you get to make, the better you feel. Every time you make a conscious choice, you are learning a valuable life skill: thinking before reacting. It's often referred to as *responding instead of reacting.* Many adults have yet to learn this valuable life skill. During your teen years is the time to really begin practicing awareness and making choices, like *who and what* to allow into your life. Making this a part of your life will give you core personal power.

YOUR THOUGHTS AND YOUR WORDS-how you talk to yourself is everything!

Please put on your big-girl panties. The butterfly- or ice-cream-cone printed ones are great! Now mentally or out loud, say this to yourself:

- "I am choosing not to answer this disrespectful text."
- "I choose to play on the computer now for 15, 20, or 30 minutes."
- "I choose not to react (or respond) to this mean or meaningless Tweet."
- Each of these is a *conscious choice.*

You totally have the power of *choice* when it comes to your thoughts and words. After you finish high school, choice becomes the number one personal power a person needs to practice to truly win at something. You can also swing to the positive by thinking, "I would like to give _____ a compliment. She had a bad day at school

Now mentally or out loud, say this to yourself:
"I am choosing not to answer this disrespectful text."
"I choose to play on the computer now for 15, 20, or 30 minutes."
"I choose not to react (or respond) to this mean or meaningless Tweet."

today." *Grow yourself up by thinking—and then talking.* This is a cool mental exercise you can do daily. Sadly, many adults don't do this very well—and I was one of them for 33 years! If you can get this down by age 21, the world will be your oyster! **Oftentimes in adolescence** we get excited about something and then feel wounded when it doesn't work out. When this happens, just be willing to ask yourself certain questions. For example, you meet someone and then wonder, "Why does this person bug me?" You will grow cooler, more understanding, and draw others to you, simply because *you thought to check in with your feelings* and then made the *choice* to send or not send that text. Taking the time to ask yourself certain questions (and then listening *inside* for an answer) will take away half your problems! It is way too easy to bad-mouth and gossip these days because of the internet.

Questions to Ask Yourself Before Posting

1. Am I trying to be popular, noticed or obnoxious?
2. Will what I am writing or about to post make me a target?
3. Am I "over-friending?"
4. Am I posting too many images of myself?
5. How much attention do I really need, and why?
6. Am I oversharing?

Am I trying to be popular, noticed or obnoxious?
Will what I am writing or about to post make me a target?
Am I "over-friending?"
Am I posting too many images of myself?
How much attention do I really need, and why?
Am I oversharing?

RECOGNIZING THE FEELING

- *Ch.14 is devoted to this *underdeveloped* human skill
- What about those disaster thoughts we all have from time to time?
  1. I am feeling like a brat. I don't like her. I'm tired of being a good girl.
  2. I'm jealous of this person.
  3. I know it could be a bit mean sharing this, but I kind of feel like posting it anyways.

Each of these is a mature recognition of *a feeling*.

When making a *choice*, it's great if you can stop and identify any *feelings* of joy, enthusiasm, anger, hurt, sadness, rejection or confusion. Identifying the feeling loosens up the power the feeling has, which is half the answer to a disturbing situation. Yippee!

Recognizing feelings is an important part of growing up. It's okay to feel angry. It's okay to feel confused. But it's important to remind yourself, when a negative feeling comes up, *The kindness I* practice *is what I will eventually receive from others.*

BECOMING MINDFUL

Acting out in anger and being a smart-mouth will always come back at you, sooner or later. I was a very quick witted smart mouth growing up. I learned the hard way, and not until after college! It does come back to bite you. I came from a family that mouthed off a lot! Mom, Dad *and* the four kids. It was a zoo sometimes. We had fun, but I wish now that we had been kinder to each other. I wish I had been reminded *repeatedly,* in a loving way by a caring adult, that meanness towards others comes back at us.

Q & A DIALOGUE TME

1. How do you speak to others?
2. How do you tweet or text to your siblings?
3. Your acquaintances?
4. Your friends?
5. Your parents?

The one really good thing about texting is it allows you to *pause and think* about your choice of words. What a great practice in choice making. In the world of psychology and spirituality, this is often called "mindfulness." Mindfulness is now being taught to preschoolers and elementary school children in progressive schools. Texting can teach us the practice of verbal mindfulness.

Example: You share with your mind by saying *silently to yourself*: "I am choosing to text Carli. I am sharing in a kind and truthful way."

TALKING, TEXTING & BOYS

This is a biggie. So many girls blow it by chasing a guy this way! Many girls mess up friendships and potential relationships by sending too many texts. I found this out when I started dating in my Second Adolescence (after my longtime marriage ended). I

Here is the number one thing to remember about texting: You cannot truly know someone or know what they are thinking or feeling through texting. It is why there are fewer real relationships developing today.

78

realized guys, young and old, are hiding behind their phones. And girls and women are allowing it! **No, no, no more.**

Here is the number one thing to remember about texting: *You cannot truly know someone or know what they are thinking or feeling through texting.* It is why there are fewer *real* relationships developing today. We all are guilty of not making real communication a priority. With mom, dad, the boyfriend or girl friend.

So often we make things up in our head because . . we will read something and then believe what we want to believe! Think about it.

- There is no voice inflection
- No eye contact.
- Is he telling the truth?
- You cannot tell if the boy is happy, sad, mad or just Horney!
- You can mis-read an emoji and it can hurt sometimes.

Words without voice inflection tell you very little. The second biggie to remember is that texting can easily chase a boy away. It is important to remember that boys like being chased . . . *for about one day.* Girls today are rarely being reminded of this. It's a big fat **CSG** (Common Sense Generalization).

There is no voice inflection
No eye contact.
Is he telling the truth?
You cannot tell if the boy is happy, sad, mad or just Horney!
You can mis-read an emoji and it can hurt sometimes.

Texting first and texting a lot is chasing!
You can text him your phone number,
but he takes it from there

TALKING ON THE PHONE - A GREAT ROMANCE PRACTICE!

We women and girls have always been the leader when it comes to helping males come out of their shell to share with us. Sadly, the easy reach of a mobile phone to text is making alot of guys these days a wimp. Self confidence builds for a male when they call on the phone. With a text... it does not. But, you have the power to guide. Its not easy and it takes some courage (and confidence) to teach males (of all ages!) how to pick up the phone and talk.

Your first action when you think you like a guy is to find out *what he is like*. You do this by *talking to him on the phone (let him call you- in most cases) or in person.* Not by texting. No excuses like, "But we texted four days straight!" Big whoop. So . . . you wash your face four days straight and that means . . . whatever. Find out for yourself *in person*: is he a nice guy or a *tell-all or tell-a-lie* guy? Talking *one-on-one* is the greatest romance practice there is. Talking on the phone is the second one. Texting for very long is lame. Here are just two reasons:

Let's say you text back and forth. Like, a lot. And then you or he says something the other takes offense at or gets turned off by. Or . . . you share so much in a text (or three) that it becomes a turn off before you have even talked on the phone together! It happens...alot.

Before you let a guy even hold your hand (don't forget, this does come before kissing) ask yourself, "Has he called me on the phone? Has he made the effort to *call me and talk* like I nicely asked him to do after those three or four texts?" Have we had a couple of fun chats on the phone? It's not that hard to redirect a guy. Remember, you are in charge. Let's say he texts you and asks to get together. YELLOW LIGHT (meaning awareness). In a very-short-and-to-the-point text, write, "Here's my number, please call me." You could also say in a sweet text, "I need to hear your voice. Call me." He will love it. You just asked him to do something he can do, a need he knows he can fulfill. Guys love that. ☺

If he can't, won't or doesn't, he is not your guy! *

IT TAKES COURAGE

Please remind yourself often that *one-on-one* talking (hearing a voice on the phone and in person) is crucial to any real success in life. From ages 12 to 18, your mindful interaction with others is the precursor to a sweet romantic future. And this does take practice. Learn this before any relationship develops. Sharing thoughtfully with others on the phone and in person is an act of self-love. Talking with others is a heart- and confidence builder. True self-esteem does not happen without it. Begin with baby steps. And yes, boys often hide behind their phones and

> Please remind yourself often that one-on-one talking (hearing a voice on the phone and in person) is crucial to any real success in life. From ages 12 to 18, your mindful interaction with others is the precursor to a sweet romantic future.

e-mails (but if we're being honest, don't we all do this?). Guiding someone to make a change like this takes courage on your part.

For centuries, boys and young men all over the world had to practice getting up the courage to look a female in the eye and share with her. A guy had to have even more courage to ask a girl out. This was done on the phone after it was invented. But she heard his voice. And she liked it. ☺ She knew he cared on some level, as she was worth the risk of asking . . . even if she did say no. It takes courage and desire for something real. Now compare that to "hooking up." No wonder guys are getting by with not committing. Guys now have the potential to get "the milk for free"; an old but important saying. And respect gets lost. Ask an adult you respect what that means.☺ Same goes for face timing. Do not let him see you .It will lesson his interest in you. Trust me.

Technology is here to stay. People today often use social media as a relationship finder. The sooner a girl establishes her own Boundaries and Standards (we will identify Values, Boundaries and Standards in Chapter 11) the easier it will be for real and trustworthy friendships and boyfriends to appear. Few adolescents and adults know how to do this. Again . . .

Raising the bar starts with you.

PHOTOS AND VIDEOS ARE THINGS!!

The most important thing you can do concerning ALL social media is this.

ASK H S (H S- holy spirit /higher self & tell mom to quit freaking out- its all good- its all God.) This inner part of you has your back!

Every time you post something ask H S,

"These words, this photo, this video will be here for life. Am I ok with this?" Then listen.

This *must do* becomes a no-brainer with practice. **If something heavy needs to be dealt with- its best one on one. But never forget** your old friend, e-mail. Some things are fine to share in an e-mail. But remember, technology stays with you . . . for life. It does not go away or get put in a drawer where no one will find it. Still aren't sure? Ask yourself:

"What about my future 11-year-old son or daughter, niece or nephew? What about my younger brother or sister?"

Recently I had a 20-year-old techie girl helping me. When I shared my book with her, she came to life, saying that she had two brothers, nine and 11 years old. She was worried about what they were being exposed to. *It starts with you.* YOU are the real celebrity. Protect yourself. Need more reasons? Check these out:

1. It's a few years later or it's next Spring. You need a j-o-b. The employer goes online and sees something distasteful. *"Sorry. You're just not a fit,"* he says.
2. You meet a wonderful guy. He decides to search for you online. He sees something questionable from years ago and thinks, "I can't bring her home to Mom." *This is real and happening to many young women today.*
3. You think you are never getting married or having children.
4. What about when you are older and the guy you have a relationship with has a young child?
5. Your future nieces and nephews who look up to you.

Count yourself lucky if you have not posted online photos that one day could come back to haunt you. If you have taken photos of yourself in a bathing suit, ask yourself:

- Why do I want to put this on the internet?
- Do I look like style and class or like a bit of a ho?
- Am I being a poser and looking hot just to show myself off?
- Do I want to look hot or cool and fine as wine?

> Why do I want to put this on the internet? Do I look like style and class or like a bit of a ho? Am I being a poser and looking hot just to show myself off? Do I want to look hot or cool and fine as wine?

This is important. Many people only know you through the internet. If you have made *smart choices* about postings, then even that mean "teen queen" who Photoshop's your head onto a naked body won't fly. Internet and live friends and acquaintances will know *your* sense of style from past postings and know something's up. How people *see* you matters. Image is not only a celebrity's number one job, it's yours too. And since you are a **real person living a real life** . . . it's that much more important.

AN EXPERT SHARES

I had the pleasure of listening to a wonderful young woman who loves social media and is a total techie. She helps the Los Angeles Police Department and kids in public and private schools all over Southern California avoid potentially life-threatening experiences stemming from misuse of the internet. Lori Getz is brilliant about navigating the internet.

She shares specific warnings with students in schools where she gives talks. I once heard her say, "It's a *black hole*. There are many dangers. Don't let yourself be fooled." I hope she will one day write a book, but until she does, here are some of her suggestions (*she knows her stuff, so suck up this info!*).

1. The key to internet safety is not drawing attention to yourself. (Hmm.)
2. There is no such thing as privacy with the internet.
3. You cannot get rid of it. You cannot control it. *("It" meaning all the information, photos and videos you or someone else posts.)*
4. Do not develop relationships online with strangers.
5. Know ahead of time (write a list) what is private to you. Now run this list by someone you respect. (This is a great boundary exercise.)
6. Memorize it.
7. Do not collect friends when you are playing online games.
8. Predators (adults who seek out young people for sex) attempt to befriend young people, oftentimes in a game rooms.
9. Create a list of what you would never post.

CREATE A WORTHY PRACTICE

Guess how one gains confidence? *By making a decision. And taking action. Its the little decisions that make life work.* Mel Robbins- a very to-the-point female life coach woke me up just hearing that.

From time to time, suggest to someone you care about that you meet in person or talk on the phone. This is a decision and an action. Bingo! Welcome to more self confidence.

From time to time, suggest to someone you care about that you *meet in person* or talk on the phone. This is a decision and an action. Bingo! Welcome to more self confidence. It's a fun life skill to practice, and you are also less likely to be talked bad about online or in school. Why? Because you have established real *one-on-one* communication. A phone conversation is a big deal nowadays. A guy who knows you, through *sharing* one-on-one communication on the phone, will think twice before talking negatively about you on a social site. If you expect honest, one-on-one communication with a boy or a friend *but do not ask for it,* you will likely not receive it. It is so worth the asking! **You will need to ask again and again.** Seriously. They don't know how to do it very well because of the tech world we are all living in.

Recently, experts have been reporting that we are all isolating and finding ourselves more alone than past generations. Without getting overly dramatic, we all need communication training, to bring back real one-on-one and group connection (phones turned OFF) to experience heartfelt human inner action. *This goes for all generations.* Your parents should practice this also. For us it's a *retraining.* Humanity needs you to help correct our culture. Many grandparents are concerned for all generations. Again . . .

*One consistent **New Action** that you*
know is in your best interest
helps more than just you.

Like what kind of action? Here are four:

1. Request a phone call by the boy before meeting up with him.
2. Call a girlfriend and say, "Hi, I feel like talking. Do you have a few minutes?"
3. Create a Yak Fest. Call three to five girls on the phone. Ask them to meet you (at the mall, outside the library, in a meeting room or the park). Just sit and yack. Important: **All *Cell* *phones off and hidden,* *before walking up to* *meet the group.*
4. Form a media club. Call it something cool, like - *Real Communicative Cuties, Film Divas.)* Now pick a movie, a Netflix show, a book - something you each have seen or read—and discuss it. Important: All phones are turned off and go into a shoebox with a lid on it!

Request a phone call by the boy before meeting up with him. Call a girlfriend and say, "Hi, I feel like talking. Do you have a few minutes?" Create a Yak Fest. Call three to five girls on the phone. Ask them to meet you (at the mall, outside the library, in a meeting room or the park). Just sit and yack. Form a media club. Call it something cool Pick a movie, a Netflix show, a book - something you each have seen or read—and discuss it.

Practicing real life *one-on-one communication* for more than 10 minutes rocks. You leave feeling fulfilled somewhere deep inside yourself. Same goes for a small group.

Gather a few girls (who like psychology and sociology). Each of you read "**How Guys Think**" (Chapter 8 of this book) or Chapter 5- **Health Facts on Sex**. Now come together and each of you read a section and start a dialogue. Share what you agreed with, a part you did not really agree with or flat out don't believe and why. Just do it!
Are you presently involved in a live group communication practice? Example: speech and debate, book club, drama group? Are you today in a group communication group? Do share your ideas on this; Go to **Girls_yourbodyisagift** Facebook Group page.

SOCIAL MEDIA REVIEW

1. Practice making conscious choices when using electronic devices.
2. Watch how much you text.
3. Choose how you respond (instead of react) to mean or meaningless social media postings.
4. Internet postings are here for life.
5. Do not develop a relationship online with strangers.
6. Ask yourself: What kind of attention? And how much attention are you asking for?
7. Texting a lot is a form of chasing.
8. Keep in mind that guys don't usually fall for the girls that chase them.
9. Remember: future employers, boyfriends and friends will see your posts from the past.
10. Make two or three phone calls. Start a conversation.
11. Sit with a friend or two once a week, with phones off and hidden from sight.
12. Call on the phone and ask four to six girls to create a Yack Fest group.

13. Call on the phone and ask four to eight girls to create a book review group, tech free.

This chapter is more important than I first realized. Please do your best to do the communication exercises.

C H A P T E R   5

HEALTH FACTS ON SEX

The more you know, the smarter you are
about waiting and choice making.

For your psychological an emotional well-being, your unique Spirit, and physical health, *information is crucial.* The consequences of young females now in their late teens and to late twenties who engaged in sexual activity while in middle and high school is not shared openly. This chapter is a brief overview of certain sexual diseases, a few statistics, and a few major FYIs most sex ed classes avoid. I would like you to understand some hidden stuff. ☺

A Cautionary Tale

Why Didn't Anyone Tell Me?

A nineteen-year-old young woman went off to college, graduated and began a full-time job. Two years after her college graduation she met and married a handsome professional man who was just a few years older. She felt blessed. The couple wanted to wait to have children.

Three years into her marriage, and close to 30 years old, she went to her annual gynecologic checkup to have a Pap smear done. During the exam, the gynecologist noticed a spot on her cervix. Two weeks later, the doctor called her and spoke with concern in his voice, "You have some abnormal cells on your cervix. We would like to freeze these cells to keep them from spreading."

The young woman was shocked. How do abnormal cells just happen? And what did it mean? She made another appointment to ask basic medical questions. Her gynecologist told her that abnormal cells found in the cervix could turn cancerous if not caught in time. She felt scared but also curious. She asked her gynecologist if the freezing of cells could keep her from having a baby. Her doctor said no, and hopefully more abnormal cells would not re-appear.

Two years later abnormal cells reappeared. The doctor thought it best to do a procedure called a conization, an in-office procedure that requires the doctor to remove a small amount of tissue from the cervix in the shape of a cone. She asked her doctor, "Will taking skin from my cervix keep me from having a baby?" "Not if only a little tissue has to be removed," replied the doctor. He knew she was determined to have children when the time was right.

The young wife was scared and frustrated. She wanted more answers. So, she asked the doctor straight out, "How did this happen?" The doctor invited her into his office and asked her to sit down. He seemed a bit hesitant. What he said shocked her. "Well, we really aren't sure . . ." and he paused before continuing. "But we (gynecologists) think that *the number* of partners a female has sexually tends to change the cells in the cervix." *Holy cow!* She thought to herself. But she had always protected herself from getting pregnant. And her intimate connections had been in loving, respectful committed relationships. She wracked her brain to put what she heard into perspective. "You mean because I had more than one lover, I have . . . whatever this is?" The doctor explained again, "Well, we aren't really sure, but we are starting to see this more and more." She walked out of the doctor's office feeling somewhat guilty and a bit stupid. Why hadn't anyone told her? Heck, even the doctor had a hard time sharing what he knew—or *thought* he knew.

Two years later the young woman found a new doctor with whom she was more comfortable. Though it did not happen easily, she became pregnant. Ten weeks later she had a miscarriage. Sad, and afraid, she asked the doctor if the conization she had two years earlier may have caused the miscarriage. "No," he stated and then added, "More women than you think experience miscarriages with their first pregnancy." She quickly became pregnant again and gave birth to a healthy ten-pound baby boy.

After her son's birth things got a bit complicated. Because of her medical history and, so there would be no chance of pre-cancerous cells returning on her cervix, the doctor suggested she have a partial hysterectomy. "What!" She sat straight up on the examining table, "I will have another baby. My son will have a brother or sister!" she blurted out. The doctor meant well, but he was hyper-sensitive, having recently had a young patient die from cervical cancer.

Twenty-one months later the young wife and mother successfully had another beautiful baby boy; a ten-and-a-half pounder at that! However, eleven months later, she followed the doctor's suggestion and agreed to have a partial hysterectomy to remove her cervix. No more children, but no more risk. She felt somehow lucky, but still confused about facts no one seemed to have.

THE END

Mother nature has always screamed the importance of sexual intimacy. But few listen. You would think the following realities of life would ring a few bells.

And the reality? Here are basics that NO ONE should take lightly:

1. Monthly periods,
2. Potential for pregnancy,
3. The responsibility of bringing a human being in to the world
4. The list of sexually transmitted diseases and infections, and, last but not least,
5. Complications of birth control.

The above realities simply have not awakened enough females. Each SCREAM in their own special way. I love the gentle *whisper of the inner knower-* the best:

Monthly periods, Potential for pregnancy, The responsibility of bringing a human being in to the world The list of sexually transmitted diseases and infections, and, last but not least, Complications of birth control.

"Hey sweet one. Your body is amazing. Your self-worth means you are entitled to real love and a real relationship. Please take your time and take THE decision to become physically intimate, seriously."

PLAN IT PLAN IT PLAN IT

PERSONAL STORY

My junior year in high school I did something that allowed me to *feel* what a huge responsibility sexual intercourse was. One day after school, I went to a gynecologist's office to support a girlfriend. As the male doctor shared, it started to sink in. I began to *understand (even feel)* how and why a female's body and sexual intercourse was an aspect of life not to be *played* with. I had no plans on being sexually active, until I was out of high school, in love and loved by a worthy and committed guy. My girlfriend (a junior also) had a college boyfriend, and she was determined to meet his needs. She had also been sexually abused.

After hearing the doctor share with her important facts on heavy sexual activity, I was glad it wasn't me asking for birth control pills. I could wait. I listened, observed, and walked away from this doctor's intelligent share, smarter and with a greater perspective on the importance of such a decision. And this was before anyone knew that the HPV virus would one day happen to 80 percent of females in the US.

*Waiting   * Planning   * Information

Though the words waiting, planning and information are not the most important words in understanding sexual intimacy, they are the **three smartest words** in sex education. The **most important** are **heart**, your **Spirit**, love, **communication** and **relationship**. And this is where many teachers and so-called experts get it wrong:

1. They do not *incorporate* the words **heart, spirit, and love**—not to mention *the human basics*—real

communication, real relationship and trust- into the curriculum.

2. They mistakenly assume you won't listen.
3. The S word and the G-word are banned in most public schools. They want to keep their job! *

> Though the words waiting, planning and information are not the most important words in understanding sexual intimacy, they are the three smartest words in sex education. The most important are heart, your Spirit, and love.

Experts, educators, and parents too often downplay sexuality by using the term "having sex' instead of saying 'physical intimacy' or "sexual activity". They discuss physical intimacy like it's going to the bathroom (like some guys think it is! Ha). Many adults seem to have *lost that loving feeling*; another great love song. (You've Lost that Loving Feeling – by the Righteous Brothers) Teens need deeper *why and how* information. You deserve to know.

The wiser the girl, the longer she will postpone sexual intimacy

WHY WAIT

Why waiting is TO YOUR ADVANTAGE

1. Your emotional maturity receives the time it needs to develop. Communication skills and playful flirting are a blast to practice in middle and high school.

96

2. Developing a real relationship and the romance dance is the bomb and it takes time! ☺ Both help you navigate and become comfortable with affection and emotional intimacy.

3. Confidence happens from having experienced a lot of sweet times without heavy sexual activity.

4. A boy walking the halls, who has been with you sexually--can create some horrible lasting feelings, and gossip may soon follow.

5. The physical health consequences of not waiting can be overwhelming years later.

6. The emotional pain a girl carries into her twenties—of having *done too much too soon*—hurts the heart, takes down her self-concept and leaves memories she would rather not live with.

7. The practice of waiting grows self-love and self-respect. "Look what you made me do" is a cop out.

Your emotional maturity receives the time it needs to develop. The guys...not so much. (important to keep in mind) Your communication skills and playful flirting are a blast to practice in middle and high school. Confidence happens from having experienced a lot of sweet times without heavy sexual activity. The emotional pain a girl carries into her twenties—of having done too much too soon—hurts the heart, takes down her self-concept

You are valuable. There is no one on earth like you. Every part of you is worth loving, respecting, and waiting for.

PLANNING IS THE BOMB

Families used to spend $20,000 and up on the wedding and reception/party for a newly-married couple who would *be consummating* their relationship. Now its "Let's hook up." What the #$@&%*!? It's because *waiting, planning* and being loved matters. And I am not talking "wait until marriage" (even though that would be the *safest* way). I know there is a "happy middle ground": *a time right for both you and him . . . a close to perfect time and way.*

It does take heart, love for self, and for each other, and a smart female to believe that she is worth waiting for. And guys love girls who know their value. Sadly, males are not aces when it comes to planning or waiting. If it's going to be . . . it's up to *you* Bu!

I hope you're ready for some gritty information, facts and figures, technical names, and a greater perspective.

SEX ED 101

FLYING UNDER THE DESK & BASIC INFORMATION

I have seen sixteen- and seventeen-year-old guys squint their eyes and pinch their mouths shut when viewing a video sharing technical information on sexually transmitted diseases. Even a demonstration of a condom being slid over a banana by the instructor can have young guys cringing! One day I saw two of them flew under their desks! **Teaching about sexuality** isn't sexy; it is simply technical and telling. In most cases, neither sex is very educated when it comes to sexual activity. Concerning those two boys under the desk, no one had shared *honestly* with them: not Mom, not Dad, not a caring relative. Boy, does it wise a guy up and slow him down when he has some facts.

THIS MAKES ME MAD

It was not until 2005 that the general public was given factual information on the most common sexually transmitted disease. In less than two decades most sexually active persons have contracted an STI or STD. It took a pharmaceutical company *willing to spend millions on research on dysplastic cells and cervical cancer* to get word out to the public. They created a vaccine for many (though not all) strains of this virus. The news finally and officially came out. It was a *virus* being transmitted that caused abnormal cells to grow. This virus is named **HPV** (human papilloma virus) and is transmitted through sexual activity. Having multiple partners increases one's risk. Still, today many teens, young adults, and their parents do not have the information they need to help them connect the dots.

Behavioral Factors Contributing to STI Transmission

STIs (sexually transmitted infections) sometimes referred to as an STD (sexually transmitted disease)

1. **Numerous sexual partners** – *more is not better*

2. **Erroneous perception of partner's risk** – meaning *mistaken, incorrect*
3. **Incorrect & inconsistent condom use. Condoms do not guarantee STI protection** -- *well duh!*
4. **No condom use** – *Russian Roulette - unless you both are virgins*
5. **Substance Abuse** – *alcohol*, *drugs, (and yes, even prescriptions!)*
6. **Sexual coercion** – *the use of force or intimidation, physical or emotional, to obtain compliance*
7. **Lack of knowledge and/or concern about STI transmission-**
8. **Other High-risk sexual behavior**
   i. **Anal intercourse-** no frigging way. Some girls are physically ruined from this act
   ii. **Oral copulation** - ditch this or save it
   iii. **Paying for sex** - Not an option
   iv. **One-night stands** – avoid at all costs

To be blunt—*anything* below the belt and unprotected . . . puts you in the unsafety, unhealthy zone.

Multiple partners greatly heighten the risk of cervical cancer.

This fact alone is one of the smartest of all the smart reasons to postpone being sexually active until after you've graduated high school, and you are in a committed, loving relationship. *The more partners you have, the greater the risk.* And yes, if your first partner has been sexually active, you are at risk. Today we

The more partners you have, the greater the risk. And yes, if your first partner has been sexually active, you are at risk. Today we know that biological changes in the cervix happen because of the HPV virus.

know that biological changes in the cervix happen because of the HPV virus. We need to keep in mind that this virus can sterilize a girl for life and left untreated, can lead to death. So yes, condoms are in order unless . . . you both are virgins, or you have both waited 6 months and been tested. If he has been with someone else within that 6-month period...you are assured of very little. And even then...its iffy. STDs are tricky. **Has anyone told you about HPV** in the way I shared it with you in the last Cautionary Tale? Wouldn't it be nice, if someone told you *how and why* cervical cancer exists? Saying "It's a virus," does not cut it. I sometimes hear girls say to me, "Oh, I got the vaccine. I'm safe." It isn't safe for her or her parents to *assume* a vaccine will cure all. HPV affects each person differently. An outside lesion may show up once, multiple times, or not at all. An STI can lead one to a lifetime of wondering when a symptom might reappear; just as with herpes outbreaks, accept that HPV can turn into cancer. **Back in 2014, Dr. Oz had a show** that stated statistical facts about women most adults are unaware of.

Eighty percent of women in the United States have or have had a sexually transmitted disease.

You read that right. EIGHTY PERCENT! Fifty percent are under age fifty. But women do not often share this, even with close friends. YOU DESERVE TO KNOW. Not knowing about sexually transmitted infections and diseases can take away your ability to create human life and can take away your own life. Females can and do die from cervical cancer.

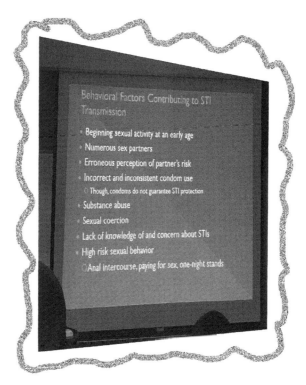

STIs
Sexually Transmitted
Diseases

ORAL SEX –DITCH IT or SAVE IT (for marriage)

Today some girls as young as eleven and twelve years old are on their knees performing sex acts done solely for the male's benefit. This very private—and unnecessary sex act had always been considered a porn thing.

Confession: **This part was hard to write.** *I don't want to hurt your feelings* if you or a friend have already done this. But I can't tiptoe around something you should know . . . but don't. This subject was in the top 3 of why my book was written. Adults don't want to share about this very touchy subject. Why? Because it *is* touchy, and most adults are not clear or willing to share about what they think or feel about oral copulation. For too long now I've sat back and watched media sell you girls on visuals of oral copulation (so not cool) and mostly for the *male viewing audience.* I have heard my share of real-life painful stories of regret from girls not too much older than you. You have a choice. Lots of them.

You knowing simple social history & health facts will help you have perspective when creating your personal **VBS** (values, boundaries and standards). Recently it has become public knowledge that males and females are getting oral cancer from performing (crazy word) a sex act that involves both the genitals and mouth. Technically it is called Felatio and Cuninlnus. I find it flat out weird that any girl today thinks she must one day have 'oral sex'. This is a highly optional act for two consenting adults in a deeply committed relationship. So, what happened?

The Clinton Scandal in 1998, VHS pornography tapes, and, finally, the internet, changed everything. Oral became the new *must do* sex act. This blew me away when a 27-year-old shared, "Well, it's just a given." Says who? She hadn't a clue that beautiful, intimate sexual relationships happen without having engaged in a B J. The very phrase, "blow job," is demeaning, and getting HPV from this optional act is the ultimate bummer. But like so much that is surfacing in the 21st century, now we have oral cancer from sexual activity. Now days, it's not just from smoking.

CDC information:

Oral cancers account for 2% to 4% of all cancer diagnoses in the United States. An oral cancer diagnosis is particularly serious; only half of the people diagnosed with oral cancer are still alive after five years, according to the CDC. In large part, because of the late diagnoses of this disease. Most signs of this cancer are difficult to detect and are often painless.
Actor Michael Douglas decided it was in the public's best interest to be forewarned. As I write this, another famous and much younger actor may be dying from oral cancer, He is not acknowledging that this is how his throat "problem" happened. At this time, he is not willing to share it. Time and honesty will tell. I always knew this optional sex act was not for everybody. But in today's hypersexualized culture... look what we have created. The newest statistics are that **70 percent are men and 30 percent are women who are now contracting HPV from oral copulation.** There are oral dams—mouthpieces a female can wear to "perform" this optional act. Stop. Before I choke on this information ☺.

STI s in Women- (Sexually Transmitted Infections

A woman's anatomy is more intricate than a man's, and this means we can be more susceptible to an STI, as there are more places for bacteria to grow more easily.

Pelvic inflammatory disease – PID

1. An infection of the fallopian tubes spread
2. PID is one of the leading causes of female infertility
3. PID is caused by some types of **STI Bacteria** – *and from being sexually intimate with the wrong person.*

Principal Viral/INCURABLE STIs

Got that? INCURABLE

A. Human papillomavirus (HPV) most common in females & males who have had multiple partners
B. The most common STI to date.
C. 20 million carriers, 6 million new cases yearly

Most types of HPV have no symptoms and cause no harm, and your body gets rid of them on its own. But some of them <u>do cause genital warts</u>. HPV infects the <u>mouth</u> and

Human papillomavirus (HPV) most common in females & males who have had multiple partners The most common STI to date. 20 million carriers, 6 million new cases yearly HPV infects the mouth and throat. Still others can cause cancer of the cervix, penis, mouth, or throat. There may be symptoms or visible warts; though many have no symptoms. Vaccines help protect both sexes from the strains most likely to cause cancer.

throat. Still others can cause <u>cancer</u> of the <u>cervix</u>, <u>penis</u>, <u>mouth</u>, or <u>throat</u>.

- There may be symptoms or visible warts; though many have no symptoms.
- Treatment and vaccine options do exist.
- Certain strains are linked to male and female cancers.
- **Vaccines** help protect both sexes from the strains most likely to cause cancer.

    Three <u>vaccines</u> (<u>Cevarix</u>, <u>Gardasil</u>, <u>Gardasil-9</u>) protect against these cancers. Gardasil and <u>Gardasil-9</u> also protect against <u>genital warts</u>, vaginal <u>cancer</u>, and <u>anal cancer</u>.

- The CDC recommends that young women ages 11 to 26 and young men ages 11 to 21 get vaccinated for HPV. A <u>Pap smear</u> shows most cervical cancers caused by HPV early on.

B. **Herpes Simplex Virus (HSV)**

- One in four women and one in eight men are infected – *this is a biggee.*
- Ulcers are painful in locations – blisters *in and around the vaginal area and around the mouth.*
- Managing symptoms – *limits sexual activity at certain times.*

C. **Hepatitis A, B, C (sometimes called Hep B)**

- A viral disease of the liver.
- Hep A is rare but is sexually transmitted.
- Transmitted mainly by blood transfusions.

- One third of Americans show evidence of past infection (YIKES).
- Hep C kills more Americans than any other disease.
- There was a 75% increase in Hep C infections between 2003 and 2016.

AIDS ANYONE? IN the 90s you died quickly having aids.

HIV/AIDS FACTS

- One In four people with HIV in the US are women
- Over 35 million people in the world live with HIV
- In the US over 1.3 million people are living with HIV
- One in eight are unaware that they have HIV

In California alone, in 2014 there were 220,543 HIV cases reported. In Ventura County, just north of Los Angeles and close to where I live, 1,224 AIDS cases were reported in 2014.

One In four people with HIV in the US are women Over 35 million people in the world live with HIV In the US over 1.3 million people are living with HIV One in eight are unaware that they have HIV

Curable STIs/Principal Bacterial

Urinary tract infections

- Often caused by several different bacteria -
- Not always sexually transmitted – *cleaning improperly*

Note: Yeast infections are not bacterial infections.

Chlamydia

Chlamydia is often asymptomatic in women, meaning there are no symptoms. Females can get **chlamydia** in the cervix, the rectum, or the throat. Men can get **chlamydia** in the urethra (inside the penis), rectum, or throat.

Chlamydia is the most reported STD in the US and is spread mostly by vaginal or anal sex, but you can get it through oral sex, too. Sometimes you'll notice an odd discharge from your vagina or penis, or pain or burning when you pee. **But it's sneaky.** Only about 25 percent of women and fifty per cent of men *get symptoms.*

- Chlamydia infects close to 3 million Americans each year.
- In 2016, close to 10 percent of all females aged 14 to 19 tested positive for chlamydia.
- In 2016, the incidence of chlamydia was 60 percent among all females 14 to 24 years of age. This is **an 86 percent increase since 2012.**

Gonorrhea

Like chlamydia, gonorrhea is often asymptomatic in women. **Gonorrhea** is a sexually transmitted disease (STD) contracted from having sex with someone who is infected with it. Some people call it "the clap." **Gonorrhea** usually causes pain and other symptoms in the genital tract, but it can also cause problems in the rectum, throat, eyes, or joints. Both men and women can get it.

- After reaching a 40-year low in 2009 Gonorrhea decreased further during 2012–2014.
- But in 2015–2016, the **Gonorrhea rate among women increased 13.8%** - 121 cases per 100,000 females.
- Close to 700,000 Americans are contracting Gonorrhea each year.
- It can cause sterility in both men and women – *meaning they are* unable to create life.
- Gonorrhea is Asymptomatic in about 20% of women and men - *meaning* no symptoms.

These two diseases have increased dramatically in the last two years.

Syphilis

Syphilis is a biggee. It scared the heck out of past generations. We believed you had to be a prostitute or pimp to get syphilis or gonorrhea. **Times have changed** due to the **promotion of pornography, unprotected sex, and a *sex-for-sex* mentality**, Syphilis has been on the rise in the US since 2001.

1. A Syphilis infection progresses in stages; a progression of infection.
2. Syphilis can lead to brain damage and death.
3. Brain damage and/or death in newborns.
4. An infection in the female can affect the fetus up to four years after she first contracted the syphilis virus.

- During 2013–2016, Syphilis increased both among men and women
- During 2015–2016, **the rate increased 14.7% among men and 35.7% among women.** These increases among women are of particular concern because as the rate of syphilis among women increases... *congenital syphilis* cases (babies born with syphilis) tend to increase.
- During 2015–2016, male, and female P&S syphilis rates increased in every region.
- Syphilis **rates increased in every age group among those aged 15 years or older** and in every race/ethnicity group during 2015–2016

Times have changed due to the promotion of pornography, unprotected sex, and a sex-for-sex mentality, Syphilis has been on the rise in the US since 2001. Syphilis can lead to brain damage and death. Brain damage and/or death in newborns. Syphilis rates increased in every age group among those aged 15 years or older and in every race/ethnicity group during 2015–2016

In recent years, MSM (Gay, bisexual, meaning men who have sex with men) accounted for the majority of reported syphilis cases in 2016. The highest rates of syphilis in 2016 were observed among men aged 20–34 years, among men in the West, and among Black men. In 2016, 27,814 cases of syphilis were reported in the United States. 8.7 cases per 100,000 population rate. This is a 17.6% increase compared with 2015 (7.4 cases per 100,000 population), and a 74.0% increase compared with 2012 (5 cases per 100,000 population).

A 74% INCREASE SINCE 2012. Helloooo!

There is nothing like a chart to wake us up to what is growing—and not for our own good.

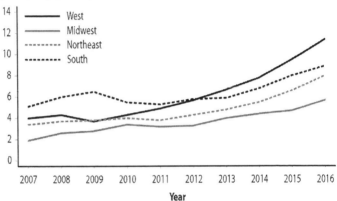

Rate of Syphilis Increase

To see more details of the above diseases - feel *free to go to the CDC Website.* Simply Google "2016 Sexually Transmitted Diseases"

A message from Sue Dunlap from L A Planned Parenthood

Picture this: A PPLA-trained sexual health educator is leading a lesson on sexual health to teens. The educator holds up a diagram of the male reproductive system and reviews the anatomy. A couple students giggle, others nod their heads. Next, the educator holds up a diagram of the female anatomy – and its complete pandemonium! This scenario is pretty common – and not just with young people. Whether in the classroom, in our health centers, or in current public discourse, there's stigma and shame around the female body.

SHE GOES ON TO SAY-

PPLA is fighting this social stigma by having honest conversations and replacing fear with facts. While not always easy, open dialogue is essential to reducing stigma and encouraging healthy sexual behavior.

CDC MEANS CENTER FOR DISEASE CONTROL

In fact, these conversations are more important than ever: a recent report from the CDC shows a sharp increase in chlamydia, gonorrhea and syphilis cases nationwide, with rates in California reaching an all-time high. Among more than 3,000 counties, Los Angeles County had the most cases of infections.

AND FINALLY

As health care providers and educators, we know people sometimes feel embarrassed or ashamed to seek testing and treatment for STIs. That's one reason we're piloting a mobile phone app, Planned Parenthood Direct, that sends STI testing kits directly (and discreetly) to patients' homes.

I know not everyone agrees with all Planned Parenthood does. You would have to be living under a rock not to know this. However, when females need honest, lifesaving information on sexually transmitted disease, medication, or birth control they do not have to feel life has abandoned them. And here's a little secret. I know personally a religious right parent (state politician) who took their teen daughter (in secret) to a Planned Parenthood Clinic - a neighboring Texas city 2 hours away from her home. Yet there were 24 clinics in the surrounding areas; *none* who provided abortion – simply reproductive health care. Go figure. **Did you know that in the 1990s, birth control and checkups were free? Yes, I said FREE.**

I put Dunlap's message in this chapter for a reason. As a young person, you knowing that these diseases **are growing nationwide** will help you and others. I taught classes on this in Texas. Our small city had the *highest STD rate* and the *highest pregnancy rate* in the *state*. **Ignorance is everywhere.** We can't blame the liberal West Coast or the Bible Belt for all of it. **We can take responsibility and wise ourselves up and help others.**

Back in the day, gonorrhea and syphilis would rarely be found in a young person. As I said earlier—there were two diseases we thought only prostitutes, pimps, and their customers could get. Oh, and pornography 'so called' actors. Things are changing, and rather rapidly. All the more reason for you to enjoy a caring communicative relationship free of heavy sexual activity. Keep your body **and your self-respect on a high level of knowing and being.** These diseases can ruin a girl's life for a while or many decades. Some sexually transmitted infections dare to take her sense of self down with it.

On a lighter note:

CONGRATULATIONS!
This was heavy and you did it!
You finished Part One!

PART 2

THE NITTY GRITTY

Take what you like and learn from the rest.

C H A P T E R   6

PORNOGRAPHY

What we are exposed to often shapes us.

A definition of pornography: *Any material or visual that portrays a human, alone or with another, engaged in a sexual activity that seems technical, intrusive, violent, rough, submissive, intruding, or controlling, that may cause arousal.*
 Over the past twenty years, pornography has exploded into everyday life . . . and has changed everything. The last two generations have not been educated (for that matter, neither have your parents) as to what pornography really is: *the misuse of the human psyche and physical body to arouse a person & make money.* Lovemaking and pornography are opposites. Self-respect and pornography are polar opposites. Stay aware of this fact.
 Physical intimacy between two caring and loving people is natural and beautiful. However, our society, with the help of today's media, has allowed human sexual activity to be restructured . . . and not for the better. What is natural and good has become a lot like the GMOs that are now in our processed food. Something has been added, and taken over, that is not naturally good for us. Greedy money-mongers, large-media corporations, adult-film companies, and the guy

down the street have taken valuable aspects of human nature, added an unnatural substance, and denigrated it. If you are conscious and caring, you can see this and feel it. And now we have bigger problems showing up. Human beings, young and old are finding hard to find have, and maintain a real and a loving relationship.

What is natural and good has become a lot like the GMOs that are now in our processed food. Something has been added, and taken over, that is not naturally good for us.

Most adolescents and people in their 20s and 30s today have an exaggerated and warped perception of sexual activity. Many young persons are viewing erotic stimuli in so many different places, they mistakenly think it is normal and that everyone should be "doing it." They have yet to experience a truly communicative, respectful, loving relationship. Many are mindlessly exploring the lower forms of human activity and diminishing their ability to experience real intimacy. Clueless in Date Land and not knowing why guys don't commit is the norm these days. It's not all an act! Both sexes deserve to see the healthier big picture. Hey, just observe the action and language on *The Bachelor*. Yikes! Great examples of what not to allow in to your life. And yes, I watch it. ☺

A FALSE BELIEF

A great many teens express the belief that abstinence and being sexually inactive is an unhealthy thing. A complete falsehood. Once a girl understands why heavy sexual relations are not ok for her, she can have a blast practicing communicating with friends—both guys and girls. This practice makes it easier for her to recognize that special someone who will forever be one of the great loves of her life. But, one must learn to share and communicate one-on-one with friends, both guys and girls comfortably first.

One-on-one and group communication practice is vitally important to a human's future work and love life. Why? It is in the times you are alone and just hanging with your friends that you begin to build a sense of self-confidence. Self-confidence does not "just happen." These interactions shape you and give you opportunities to find out who you want to be as a person. Being with a guy all the time can change you into someone you don't know. And that someone is *you*! It's tricky.

RESEARCH ON PORNOGRAPHY & TEENS

Researchers discovered in a study that prolonged exposure to pornography breeds cynicism about love and the need for affection. It also breeds a belief that marriage is sexually confining. The idea of starting a family and raising kids starts to lose attraction. Kind of sad, isn't it? Researchers studying the effects of pornography have started to see some unnatural (and unsettling) trends:

1. Increased appetite for more and more graphic images and sexual activity associated with abusive, illegal, or unsafe practices.
2. A large rise in the number of people who are struggling with addictive and sexual behavior.
3. A sharp rise in cases of infidelity.

In 2012, five different studies examined the connection between pornography consumption and commitment to a romantic relationship. The researchers in all five studies concluded that the more pornography that was seen, the more weakened the commitment is to a relationship. (Covenant Eyes, p. 12.) **A study done** by the University of Alberta on students between ages 14 and 17 surveyed how often teens accessed sexually explicit media. Ninety percent of boys and 70% of girls reported accessing it on at least *one* occasion. Thirty-five percent of boys said they had accessed such sites "too many times to count." Another study of 14- to 17-year-olds—conducted in 2008—found that 58% of teens said they had never seen pornography, but this was a while back. However, the same study found that 71% of sexually active teens have viewed pornography, 42% of sexually active teens viewed pornography regularly, and more than a quarter of boys used pornography once a week. Keep in mind that cell phones were only just starting to become like a backpack for middle schoolers.

JOURNAL TIME

1. What do you think new statistics almost a decade later would reveal?
2. How many tweens and teens (girls and boys) today who are *not sexually active* do you think have been exposed to pornography? 10%? 30%? 50%? 75%?
3. Do you believe watching pornography increases one's desire to be sexually active?
4. What positives in society do you think pornography contributes to?
5. What negative aspects of our society today do you think pornography contributes to?
6. Remember . . . when this study was done, cell phones were only *just starting* to become as common among middle schoolers as a backpack.

You are the first generation where parents are being urged to discuss pornography with you. Right . . . urged? By who? Educators have yet to create classes or seminars that actually get real about ALL the crud you are exposed to. What schools or school districts are brave enough to share and educate you? *The problem is they have not had the time to regain a healthy objective perspective and share healthy solutions to what is now an epidemic.* Most educators are afraid they will lose their job. Share with them your thoughts. *Your thoughts matter.* You just may have to clue adults in a little. One thing they *do know* that you may not: they have seen marriages break up because of a husband's addiction and preoccupation with pornography. This stuff is real and is breaking families apart.

> What schools or school districts are brave enough to share and educate you? The problem is they have not had the time to regain a healthy objective perspective and share healthy solutions to what is now an epidemic.

I guess what I'm getting at is how massively important it is for you to make a conscious effort to stay clear of sexually explicit pornographic media. Your present and future psychological well-being and romantic relationships depend on it. It takes very little to warp what Mother Nature meant to be special.

JUST DO IT

Your quick response in turning away from pornographic anything *is crucial.*

When someone throws "it" in your face at school (on a phone), Put up your hand. Pivot and maybe flip your hair!☺ Same goes for when you see a raunchy cable or network show, computer crud, and for sure the gross movie titles on the cable TV guide screen. Personally, I think cable TV should be sued just for posting the disgusting titles. Hmm, wanna help me? Let's review this again. Say something deeply offensive shows up...

Take a deep breath and do 2 of the following

- Flip the channel.
- Click the mouse elsewhere
- Turn off the tech gadget
- Get up and start dancing (check my music list & YouTube one)

Say something deeply offensive shows up.
Take a deep breath and do 2 of the following
Flip the channel.
Click the mouse elsewhere
Turn off the tech gadget
Get up and start dancing (check my music list & YouTube one)

Choose one of the above when you have pornography thrown your way. Why? It changes your energy *away* from what hurts the human heart and psyche. Remember when I said, "Your not a guy"? And not that all guys like pornography. Many males are starting to wake up to its damage. The *day will come that you will thank me. Why? Because you protected your heart and attracted someone* worthy of you; someone who will likely be as healthy as you. Like attracts like, right? This is important and a practice you will be **super grateful** you did as you get older.

VIOLENT AT ITS CORE

One of the most important things to remember is most pornography has violence and/or control at its core. Researchers argue on the percent of violence and submission in pornography. The best guesstimate is between 70 and 90 percent. But most agree that pornography is often disguised as something else. That something else is *control,* usually of women. How do young women and girls today feel about this? Why are they not protesting? Instead some are playacting like a porn queen or acting like a guy. Great. What a wonderful contribution to society . . . not.

> One of the most important things to remember is most pornography has violence and/ or control at its core. Researchers argue on the percent of violence and submission in pornography. The best guesstimate is between 70 and 90 percent.

Pornographic visuals are so easily available that many young people think it's an OK way to relieve themselves sexually. However, studies show that frequent viewing creates an addiction, causing a multitude of sexual problems for teens, adult males, and married men who view pornography often.

> Pornographic material is blunt, crude, and devoid of relationship. It degrades all human sexual activity. A psychological and physical dysfunction develops, warping the viewer's capability to experience real lovemaking and physical intimacy.

Pornographic material is blunt, crude, and devoid of relationship. It degrades all human sexual activity. A psychological and physical dysfunction develops, warping the viewer's capability to experience real lovemaking and physical intimacy. Consistent pornography viewing wipes out an understanding of what a loving relationship is and . . . *a natural act in its perfect and right time becomes unnatural.*

The pornography industry is sneaky. Mild pornography is sometimes referred to as "soft porn,". They soften up the storylines of their cheap movies to entice the viewer. Recently, a movie that was full of pornographic scenes won an Academy Award. No one in Hollywood or on the TV talk shows mentioned that many scenes were pornographic. Do you know why? The television networks were receiving money from advertising. The talk show hosts would have lost their jobs if they had mentioned it. The actors were reputable, and so it passed as a normal movie. Well, ha ha. The joke is on all of society, growing children, adolescents, parents, and even your children someday. Please keep this in mind.

Ft. note: Interesting that during the Judge Kavanough fiasco in the fall of 2018, he blamed heavy drinking while in highschool on movies; he named Animal House and Fast Times at Ridgemont High. Excuse me. He graduated in 1982. Fast Times came out in August of 1982. He had all ready graduated.

Q & A DIALOGUE TIME

1. Can you name two movies that you know have pornography in them and yet our culture now shows them as "normal?"
2. Name two television or cable shows you believe have pornography in them.
3. Are you aware that you have every right to **see and feel things** as you **see and feel** them - and not as media wants you to see them?

*The act of acting morally is behaving as if
everything we do matters.*

Gloria Steinem

Girls Who Make the Choice to Go Unconscious

Pornography damages people from all social classes, from addiction to total sexual dysfunction of the male. But let's start with the females involved. Many girls in the pornography industry come from backgrounds of sexual abuse. These girls sometimes share that they're often not able to feel or to trust another human being. Feeling and caring is the last thing a pornography actress/victim can afford to do. A girl's feelings (her heart and Spirit connection) need to be blocked in order to perform sex acts in front of a camera crew. Years later, these young women wake up to feeling the effects of having been *used.* A great many of them consume alcohol and drugs during pornography film shoots. Disease and addiction follow these women long after they've moved out of this work. Bottom line . . . pornography is an industry that would best be *nuked.*

Victims of pornography do not see that they are contributing to the ongoing *violence and disrespect* of *all* women. While she becomes emotionally warped, she contributes to warping our world. **The pornography industry exists to make money and is the largest contributor to sex trafficking of girls worldwide.**

The Pornography Industry

- Generates control of women,
- Contributes to violence against women,
- Generates worldwide sex trafficking
- Increases the demand to sell and buy young girls and women.

Q & A DIALOGUE TIME

1. Were you aware that pornography is, at its base, violent and controlling?
2. Did you know that pornography is an eight-billion-dollar-a-year business?
3. How do you think pornography and the sex trafficking of young females is linked?
4. What do you think causes people to care more about money than people?

> Pornography generates control of women,
> Contributes to violence against women,
> Generates worldwide sex trafficking
> Increases the demand to sell and buy young girls and women.

EDUCATE YOUR PARENTS

Our society has allowed pornography to slide into American culture and media, even without the internet. The blatant sex scenes in movies today are a first. And very recently even our four major networks, NBC, CBS, ABC, and Fox, not just cable, are allowing it. This new reality has many parents and grandparents not wanting to talk about s-e-x or even watch TV at all. Count yourself lucky if you have a willing parent to share with. Please remind yourself that all this *pornography gone mainstream* is new to them too. Truth is, what is really a private human experience is now being displayed just as easily as you would turn on a faucet.

Many parents today have grown up with *teen sex movies* and *Cosmopolitan magazine.* Too many parents today are unaware that they too have been slowly conditioned to disconnect LOVE from physical intimacy. But exposing children and teens to pornography is a whole new, sad reality. You have very little PG (parental guidance) protection. *You must be the grown-up here* if you desire a beautiful, authentic love life in your life one day. Give them a break, and yourself too, for not knowing. But now, you know. And you know to take action. Maybe ask them this:

> *"Hey mom, what television shows do you think show unacceptable stuff, like sex scenes that have no respect or relationship in them, but they are on a TV screen in our living room?"*

I'd love to be a fly on the wall to hear your parents' answers. ☺

A Heart and Mind Practice

Sometimes we stumble upon a P scene: *rough, quick, mechanical, and thoughtless physical scenes.* Here's a truth that a parent would have a hard time sharing with you, but you should know it. Re-enacting these scenes in real life would be unpleasant at best. But how does a mom or dad tell you this without turning ten shades of red? They don't. But you need the info. Because sometimes people do stupid things like try and imitate a movie scene. And then feel yucky and tricked. This happens way too often.

Actors often admit how uncomfortable these scenes

Many young women are thinking and acting like a guy when it comes to engaging in sexual activity! Too often the guy comes to mistake the girl for a "ho". She is acting out from her limited knowledge, experience and misinformation.

are to film. But now many young women are thinking and acting *like a guy* when it comes to engaging in sexual activity! Too often the guy comes to mistake the girl for a "ho,". She is acting out from her limited knowledge, experience and misinformation. She acts out what she sees in media! **It is *so not natural* for a female** to approach physical intimacy the way a young man is able to. How do I know? Experience, time and reflection. Most women today are not taking the time needed to reflect honestly with themselves. So how do they teach *you*? Some rely on religious beliefs when sharing. But as a teen you know something is not making sense.

We females love real communication,
relationship, romance, and love.
And should settle for nothing less.

How do I know this for sure? Well for one, I have lived it and have received honest feedback from guys today. Check this!

A STORY TALE

Doing It Right in High School

One day as I was feeding my youngest son a bottle and feeling like Freeda Frump. A guy who I dated my Sophomore and Junior year of high school, off and on, called me. He was 3 years older and had been a big football player at a major university. He was actually my date my Sophomore year for Homecoming. He asked me how I was. It was kind of weird. Heck, it was 20 years ago! I was married and living 1,200 miles away from where we had gone to high school.

He starts sharing about how much fun he had just kissing and making out on my parent's sofa. I started turning red. He then, out of the blue adds, "Heck, we didn't even do anything. And I still remember how much fun it was." Yikes! Though I was embarrassed, I felt good, actually thrilled that he still thought of me and those high school dates. This is what I mean when I say *our past does come back up…when we least expect it!*

The End

Too many girls today are willing to settle for less

PORNOGRAPHY TODAY IN TEEN LIFE . . .

The *getting-on-her-knees* thing

The pornography industry has always used oral copulation as *the suggested* standard visual to entice the male fantasy trigger. Let me repeat this: *to entice the male fantasy trigger. This act was often* shown in men's pornography magazines and adult films. So when the president Clinton sex scandal hit, it blew the minds of parents of tweens and teens. Many parents since that time have stayed in denial that it would ever become 'a thing'. Megann McCain, on The View in 2018 shared that this is how she learned of oral copulation. Yes, she, my sons, and most tween and teens in the U. S. got a huge OMG with a *first of its kind* presidential sex scandal. Because I was a sex educator I could not stay in denial. Chapter 8 shares my own experience with 2 very open tweens.

Remember this: The girl who thinks simulating pornography is cool…loses out on experiencing human intimacy/real lovemaking. I have had girls in their early and mid-twenties share with me feelings of deep regret, and that today they are dealing with major damage to their self-worth. I want their experiences shared, but because of the graphic nature of their stories, I have chosen to share only one Cautionary Tale in Chapter 8 on this subject.... a middle school tale no less.

It is not fair to any girl to not share
with you the bigger picture.

Most adults will not talk about this. It's too intimate, too personal. They know it's happening and admit it's making them crazy. We are now seeing it suggested on certain television shows. Pornography gone main stream. How low can we go values wise?

In the long run, pornography gone
mainstream serves no one.
Not even the horny teen guy.

You having information from a caring adult is *pure power,* not a permission slip. Parents have a hard time believing this for lots of reasons. But in today's world *they must do their best.* And you saying, "Don't talk to me about sex!" is not helping. My boys said the same thing. Today, they are grateful I shared with them and dragged them and their friends to sex ed workshops during their middle school years. Just keep this in mind: *nothing is as it seems, especially if it's shown in the media.* You have power when you have the facts and can be attuned to what *feels right* inside. Do not let anyone take this personal right away from you.

PHYSICAL DAMAGE TO BOYS

The damage to boys and men from pornography is epidemic and is destroying the ability of many young males to intimately communicate and to be affectionate. They start to confuse affection with sex and have a harder time with the simple practice of romance. And now girls are sometimes doing this too. To function naturally in life, we all need to practice communicating, romancing, and flirting way before making *real* love.

As a result of being exposed to pornography, boys are having a hard time discovering what a caring relationship is. <u>Girls, you are the teacher—the leader in love, if you will.</u> Girls always have been. So, what happened? Well besides the cell phone, texting, and pornography in all forms of media...

> The damage to boys and men from pornography is epidemic and is destroying the ability of many young males to intimately communicate and to be affectionate. They start to confuse affection with sex and have a harder time with the simple practice of romance.

A relationship starts with respectful communication and romance, not sexual activity.

Sexual addiction is real. I recently had a twenty-six-year-old young woman tell me that at age 12 ½ she became addicted to reading erotic novels on her cell phone. She spent a year and a half with a psychologist because of her addiction to physically acting out. All of this, I believe, is due to using pornographic media to experiment and to avoid one's own thoughts and real feelings.

Masturbation has always been around. Decades past, guys would use a magazine, or their imagination. Even looking at a centerfold, though, most guys had a basic respect for a female. Today they are seeing girls on a screen that make it hard for them to desire the *real deal: communication, affection, relationship, and love*. Today pornography is blowing it for males and warping many females of their natural desire to one day make love (not 'have sex') and be respected. Never take less. *Hey, you're in charge!*

RAISE THE BAR

Please remember, *always trust your feelings, and then use common sense*. A thinking-feeling practice alone allows you to know *naturally* that making love and pornography are polar opposites in feeling, content, and form.

1. *Content*—pornography has none.
2. *Feeling*—pornography has none.
3. 70% to 90% percent of pornography is violent and/or degrades the female.
4. *Form*—pornography penetrates, intrudes, and controls the other. It is usually crude and rough and can be violent in composition and content.

WHAT YOU LET IN – YOU BECOME

If someone shows you anything pornographic, on a phone, a computer, a smart pad, or television you now know how to protect yourself.

1. You are worth guarding your heart, mind, and Spirit.
2. You are strong enough to turn away and tell the person to back off or take a hike.

This is personal power and an act of self-love. A cool response to blocking anything pornographic will only strengthen your sense of self and your future love life. Be different. Different is good. By different I don't mean dressing sleazy. I was different, and I dressed in amazing ways. It was good, and very good in helping me feel good about me. The sad joke is . . . most kids don't want to be different. Oh, yes you do. It's what makes you cool. It is what makes you unique. It also *feels* better. Others may wonder where you are coming from. But it shows those who are afraid to be themselves that they, too, can make wise choices, be cool, and help change our whacked-out world.

> You are worth guarding your heart, mind, and Spirit. You are strong enough to turn away and tell the person to back off or take a hike. This is personal power and an act of self-love.

Remember, it starts with you.

.

C H A P T E R   7

ALCOHOL, DRUGS, CIGARETTES, VAPING & OTHER MIND NUMBERS

We were born to feel. What we do with our feelings is part of the art of living.

Drinking and and/or using drugs are causing mega problems for teens. Research says 70% of teens have used alcohol, marijuana, and or prescription drugs. Far too often, girls are doing unthinkable sex acts because they are using alcohol and/or drugs. Often a girl will drink and/or use drugs, so she won't feel what she may be *getting ready to do* physically with a boy. Becoming a bit numb or unconscious (a primary reason for using) allows a girl *to not think* about what she is doing. It's lame and happens way too much.

A CAUTIONARY TALE

Blowing It Early

Joni, a junior in high school, decided she could drink . . . even though drinking was against her parents' home rules and illegal in her state. In mid-October, she began to drink every other weekend. By the end of November, it was every weekend. She also began smoking marijuana when it was offered to her. In December, she started blowing off classes and partying during the week, using alcohol and marijuana. By Valentine's Day, she was missing most of her classes and ragging on her parents daily. Her drinking and using was crushing them.

Soon, Joni's family was living in daily chaos. Her younger brother and sister were often pushed to the side as mom and dad spent time worrying over their often drunk or stoned daughter. Joni was in her own world. She did not care who she was hurting.

By spring break Joni experienced an emotional (drug-induced) breakdown. She was sent off to an expensive rehab, not covered by insurance. Her parents were forced to use her college savings to pay for the treatment center. She missed her junior prom, her friends, and the second semester of her junior year. Her spring break and spring semester were a complete wash. Upon her return home from rehab, she spent six to ten hours a week in twelve-step meetings: her new place for learning how to live life clean and sober.

Joni made the choice to drink while in high school. She blew the money she could have had for college. But worse than money was the time missed. One's junior year is special. You are now an older teen: a time when experiencing social interactions allows you to dig into the practice of honoring boundaries, both emotional and physical. Joni missed valuable time needed to learn the practical life lessons that would prepare her for adulthood.

THE END

There was much about love and life Joni could have experienced but did not. Instead, she spent her adolescence working on staying sane and sober. To be an addict or a drunk during your teen years is one tough road. Warning: be conscious of the genes you've inherited. If you have a parent or grandparent dealing with excessive alcohol or drug use, you are more susceptible to substance abuse yourself.

FIRST EXPERIENCES

Have you ever had a boy take your hand, hold it, and you had no idea he was going to do this? What about the first time you experienced watching a movie with a boy you liked a lot? Imagine him putting his arm around you. How might that feel? What about that first kiss from someone you're crazy about? Can you imagine (or remember, for older girls) that sweet lip press on your cheek or lip kiss from a guy you really like? How will (did) that feel? What about the charge of electricity going through you . . . like *completely!* You are happy.

Guess what. You can kiss these first *one-of-a-kind* life experiences goodbye should you decide it's easier to get drunk or stoned as a young teen. "But whyyyyyyyyyyyyyyyy?" whines the little Valley girl.

The purpose of alcohol and drugs is to numb out, a little or a lot. That natural electrical charge from a first experience will have a major glitch in its circuit after one drink or hit of something (like weed). Weed may come from the earth and wine from grapes, but the pure natural charge of a kiss or handhold is a *natural high* that will be missed should a girl feel the need to get buzzed. You simply miss out.

Real feelings—the natural highs of life's firsts, seconds, and thirds—are for too many girls today a pipe dream. You miss the boat, so to speak. The alcohol, the joint, or the prescription drug blocks it. Using is a *choice*. Again, if you have a family history of heavy alcohol or drug use, your days may be numbered. Here's a fact. Marijuana is not what it was in the hippie days. Not even close. The strength of weed today is 28 to 40 percent higher. What does this mean? It means its time to wake up to the following:

> Real feelings—the natural highs of life's firsts, seconds, and thirds—are for too many girls today a pipe dream. You miss the boat, so to speak. The alcohol, the joint, or the prescription drug blocks it. Using is a choice.

1. Family history of using and addiction greatly increases your risk.
2. Marijuana today is so strong that playing like a hippie-chick from "back in the day" isn't an option (but hey, you *can* dress like one☺ & its more fun)
3. Prescription drugs are the number-one addiction of adolescents today.

Let's use a friend as an example. Maybe she didn't have the confidence, or strength of character to just hang out or go to a party at someone's house and be fully conscious. Or what about a girlfriend who thought it a bright idea to find an illegal substance or pop a pill it so she could feel loaded?

It does take brains, thinking before acting (mindfulness), self-will and an inner confidence. Not confident enough? Fake it till it becomes your reality. Say "Nope" or "No thanks," or "No way, I'll pass," again and again. You are now acting consciously. Let that sink deep in you. Half of all adults are not conscious. Staying conscious builds your self-confidence. This is a level of being in your *mind and heart* nobody can take away from you. You are not just saying no because it's illegal and you could get hurt or caught. It's a big friggin' deal to stay conscious. You will treasure certain memories all your life. I know because I have lived it. And to this day . . . those memories rock. Sadly, my very best friend from sixth grade (the other cheerleader in Chapter 1), drank for the first time the summer after ninth grade. She has spent a lifetime battling heavy addictions. She has what AA calls the *allergy of addiction.* Her chemistry is perfectly wired to stay drug dependent. I love talking to her. But much of what I vividly remember she does not. Though clean and sober today, many of her memories are a fog. Life has been hard for her.

You will never have the chance, in this lifetime, to relive or remember how cool a real first kiss is or the many experiences of affection you can have should you allow yourself to be influenced by a fun-loving but misguided group of friends.

STAYING CONSCIOUS

Staying conscious does something else that rocks. It helps you increase the social skills and the confidence you need to finish school and do well in life. Do not blow this unique time in your life. You will be so darned grateful for the rest of your life that you didn't fall on the grass, throw up with mascara running down your face at a party and have a video taken of you and then posted on a social media site (for life). **Guys hate looking at girls** who are loaded. However, less-than-honorable guys don't mind using girls who get loaded. ☺ It is up to you on how you choose to show yourself to others in public. If you think being one of the gang and getting drunk or high is cool, how you experience life will become quite difficult. Tell me: who needs their life to be *more* difficult and confusing? Your little self is saying "I do, I do!" Your Higher Self (connected to your unique Spirit) is saying, "Please . . . I love you so much. Just chill. I promise, I have better plans for you!" The *little self* (I like to call her Garianna) and your Higher Self will be explained in Part 3.

Guys hate looking at girls who are loaded. However, less-than-honorable guys don't mind using girls who get loaded. ☺ It is up to you on how you choose to show yourself to others in public.

Here are some facts:

- Alcohol and nicotine are drugs.
- Cocaine, heroin, bath salts, hash, spice, marijuana, and prescription drugs are all drugs. They alter the mind.
- Seventy percent of teens today abuse alcohol before they finish high school.
- Forty percent of these teens will have abused other illegal substances before finishing high school.
- More teens die from prescription drugs than from cocaine and heroin combined.

All adolescents are highly vulnerable to the effects of drugs. Your brain is not fully developed. The effects of a substance last longer, and you also go to rehab quicker. You are not an adult yet and you are affected in dramatic ways that can damage your developing brain.

Here's an FYI about *using* while in high school. You are in school not just to learn academics, but also social skills with girlfriends, potential boyfriends, boys that are friends, and adults. *When you are getting high, even a little, you stop learning.* Check this! This is scary.

> You are in school not just to learn academics, but also social skills with girlfriends, potential boyfriends, boys that are friends, and adults. When you are getting high, even a little, you stop learning.

THE DAY a girl (or guy) starts drinking or drugging, and it becomes a problem (as in addiction—known or not known) is the day she stops maturing emotionally. This means if a girl is 15 when she first starts using heavily, even on her 35th birthday, she is still fifteen-year-old emotionally. Yikes! I know a forty-five-year-old who is living proof.

The goal and the gift to yourself is to stay conscious in social situations, to keep from looking like an idiot and doing things you will regret. *This also grows your self-esteem alot. But most important,* and rarely shared is the potential for emotional stuntedness if you use alcohol or drugs during your developing years. On a personal note, I will tell you something my oldest told

> The goal and the gift to yourself is to stay conscious in social situations, to keep from looking like an idiot and doing things you will regret. This also grows your self-esteem alot.

me. He said it was the best thing I shared with him. Now, I don't believe many parents would have said what I said *like I said it* . . . but here goes: *"Whatever you do,"* I told him, *"don't drug and drink in high school. Should you become an addict you will totally blow your fun college days." He took the advice to heart and waited to party in college. And yes, he easily made up for it. And I thought it was my lessons on girls, love and dragging him, his younger brother, and their friends to sex ed classes on Saturdays that he so loved and appreciated!* I love the 12-step slogan for family members of addicts

THINK   THINK   THINK

C H A P T E R   8

IT'S NOT REALLY SEX

OUR CULTURE'S DISTORTION OF SEX & INTIMACY

A CAUTIONARY TALE

HORSE CAMP & MORE

Once upon a time two cute tween brothers, Jason and Patrick, went to a really cool summer horse camp for kids ages eight to eighteen. This camp was coed. The girls and guys would roam around and mingle together for two weeks on a large horse ranch. On the last Saturday evening, something shocking happened. It was one of those things that if parents found out about, they might try to sweep under the rug. But no one learns that way. So, here goes!

It was a Saturday evening. The two-week camp session was technically over. Most of the camp counselors had gone into the nearby little Texas town for some fun: a short break before meeting the new campers who were due to arrive the following morning. Patrick and Jason's parents had driven into town that morning and were staying at a nearby motel. A few of the young campers were still at camp this particular evening. Jason, the soon-to-be sixth-grader asked his parents to let him stay on the campground one last night with three of his older brother's camp buddies. What Mom and Dad didn't know was that most of the camp counselors had gone into town.

That evening Jason walked into the unsupervised rec room to find his brother's friends. Much to his surprise, he saw Darcy, a cute blonde (braces and all), down on her knees "doing" Donny! On the long drive home, this information and more was shared. Darcy *performed* this sexual act three times with Donny over the next few days. The following Wednesday Donny broke up with her. He met a new girl at camp.

THE END

I sometimes wonder how Darcy, now in her early 30s, feels about herself. Had she seen former President Clinton on TV saying, "I did not have sexual relations with that woman?" Is this what influenced her? Maybe deep down this soon-to-be eighth-grade girl was feeling unworthy or unpopular. Was she lacking a sense of value? She came from a well-educated family. Her parents obviously cared for her, as her mother had been seen at the campground that morning washing her daughter's clothes for the following week. Truth be told, many highly educated people fare no better in discussing necessary information about sexual intimacy. Her parents grew up with love & passion in music (rock, soul and slow) and naturally connected romance and relationship with sexual intimacy. It was a no brainer. They expected her to do the same. But it was all changing. In 1998 parents were just beginning to see *sex everything* in media and internet pop ups. One simple question you might ask yourself...

Why do I think Darcy allowed this to happen?

As an adult- here's my *go to*. Maybe her mother and father simply forget to tell her (like repeatedly) that she was valuable and that her body was a gift, that guys are to honor and respect her. Perhaps they *thought* their love for her was enough. Apparently, she did not know she was a treasure. There is a good chance that how she behaved in her middle school years has come back to haunt her.

WHAT WE DO MATTERS

Even in our early years on this planet.

Shortly after the Clinton scandal young, misguided- and *zero*-guided girls started engaging in an activity that many couples don't consider part of their intimate relationship. Some girls today don't believe me when I share this with them. Let's get something straight: oral sex is sex. I believe a majority of women (I'm guessing close to 70 percent) in the real world could care less about this sex act. Oral copulation is not on all married or single couples' sexual intimacy list. But it is still a sexual act. I'm guessing more than half of all women never want to perform (crazy word, but pornography is *performance*) this act.

I heard something funny the other day. I shared the story with a psychologist. She simply stated," Hey, it's a *job*. Why do you think they call it a *blow job*? (Sorry mom or loving trusted adult reading this. Not talking is hurting us all) ☺

Young adult males and grown men say they prefer not to be asked to reciprocate (google "reciprocate"). Did you know that people in general rarely discussed the act of oral sex until the Clinton scandal brought it into the forefront of popular culture in 1998? The pornography world has always used this act to entice males to buy pornographic media. And now it in the air waves thanks to internet access. **All girls need** to know this. Why? Because girls for the last twenty years have been tricked. They have bought into a horny guy's fantasy that it's a must. Ha! No, it's not. Girls and women under forty have somehow been made to believe this sexual act is a *must do*. As a girl, you are in charge. If this act does not sound or feel right for you . . . guess what? It's not. You have the freedom and responsibility to call the shots. **Think about this.** Until the Clinton scandal, committed couples had free choice (and it *is* a *choice*) to partake in this very intimate act, a sexual act that *is still best left private, as in it is only the couple's business.* The statement that "oral sex is not really sex" is false. What the President should have said was, "I did not have sexual intercourse with that woman." We can't totally blame him for saying it wasn't sex. Heck! *He may have believed this!* Why? Because it does not happen between all married or committed adult couples. Oral sex is not even listed as a base in the "baseball theory!" (More about the "baseball theory" in Chapter 10). It simply is not a desired sexual act by all human beings. But now, it is the latest *must do* act? No, it is not; far from it.

I refuse to be politically correct. I've heard too many girls in their 20s and early 30s today share stories of regret telling me they are *still* confused. Historically and socially speaking, up until the Clinton scandal it was known on high school campuses …that it was the girl who couldn't get the guy that 'performed" this act. Well, it looks like a lot of girls these days aren't getting the guy anyway. So . . . ditch it or save it for marriage. **I promise** you won't lose a worthy guy over not "performing" this act. Do not be surprised if you lose more than the guy, if you do.

Confession: **This was hard to write**. *I don't want to hurt your feelings* if you or a friend have already done this. But I can't tiptoe around something you should know . . . but don't. **For the last twenty years** it's been happening between middle schoolers more and more often. Yes, under school stairwells, in bathrooms, under tables at bar mitzvahs, and beneath bleachers at football games. It kind of makes you want to throw up . . . or wise up. Take your pick.

Adults don't want to share about this very private act. Why? Because it *is* private, and most adults are not clear about what they think about it. Many adults have messed up in their own lives, so they really don't want to talk about it. For too long now, I've sat back and watched media increase what it sells you girls false visuals of not just oral but rough and tough quickie sex scenes that again are mostly for the *male viewing audience*. You have a choice. Got this? It's no surprise that things are so out of balance...all the way up to Washington D C.

YOU ARE ONE-OF-A-KIND WONDERFUL

Give yourself a break and boost your self-esteem. Never NEVER buy into a guy's wants or fantasies.

I recently asked a very intelligent fifteen-year-old girl, who lives in the South, "Why do you think some girls do this? Why do some girls lower themselves for an act that provides no benefits for them, and degrades their moral character?" She said, "I think

> You need never go out of your way or break your personal boundaries to "pleasure a guy sexually." Never, ever, and never. Spending time with you is enough.

they just want to pleasure the guy." Hmm . . . Really? I wonder why. **You need never go** out of your way or break your personal boundaries to "pleasure a guy sexually." Never, ever, and never. *Spending time with you is enough.* A guy you are interested in, and who is truly interested in you, should be swimming a river for you. If he won't, he is not the guy for you. Remember, *YOU* are the prize. *YOU* are the gift. Apparently, some girls forget this. You are one-of-a-kind wonderful, unique and special in your own way. You are beautiful inside and out and you deserve the highest amount of respect. Unless . . . you choose to "ho out."

Oral sex is not a harmless act. If you have a friend who has convinced herself that it "isn't really sex," the day will come when she will cringe thinking of her past and regret having done it. This sexual act can destroy a girl's social life and her friendships with other girls. But, more important, her actions can slowly eat away at her self-worth, leaving her with horrible feelings about herself. A 24-year-old shared with me at Magic one day (Magic is THE high-end fashion market held twice a year). She said she feels shame today, ten years later, but she was excited about this book. She said that she did not want young girls today to do what she did. When a girl does not know what she *feels,* she may do regrettable acts. Part of her has cut off from feeling; from connecting to her heart and Spirit.

Be a friend. If you know someone who has made this mistake, ask her, "What is the upside to oral sex?" Was it because afterward he smiled and patted her on the head? Now she gets to wonder if he will ever call her or even say hello to her at school.

Do you know what you think and feel about this do-all-tell-all sex act? Remember this: Some women grow into it.

Many women do not. Sorry guys! Then again, not all guys *really* care about what women want.

Recently some older guys shared their personal opinions with me. I had a thirty-something guy say to me, *"I am very careful about ever doing this act with a girl. Mostly I choose not to . . . too much risk of disease."* And what one guy shared (after I mentioned this chapter with him) shocked me. I will quote his exact words. *"Well, it is kind of degrading for the girl, but we like it."* I wanted to slap him. Instead, I put his share in my mental savings account.

Keep your Standards and Boundaries high and close to your heart. Keep growing your own unique and greater sense of self.

JOURNAL TIME - What Do You Think?

1. Why would a girl perform this act?
2. How do you think girls who have performed this act feel?
   Proud?   Disappointed?   Numb?   don't care?
3. Why would a girl who has done this act say, "It's no big deal" or "I don't care?"
4. What do you think a boy might think about girls who perform oral sex?

Many young girls today simply lack *honest information and a way to* ask themselves the important questions. Asking yourself certain questions is how you create guidelines and boundaries. But even adults, who know they have values, and standards (somewhere)... have a hard time actually identifying their own VBS.

A GOLDEN FEELING LESSON

Next time something weird happens, or you hear about it having happened . . . STOP. Ask yourself, "What am I feeling?" Feelings are not right or wrong. But when it comes to physical intimacy and love, you will like *you* better if you can identify the feeling. And it gets tricky. *Sometimes something can feel good but not right.* Your personal responsibility is to take the time to **feel and then think** things through. **Honor your thoughts** and feelings through your *words and your actions.* No matter what the people around you, or the media talking heads, are saying or doing, stick to your beliefs if they *feel* right to you.

> Honor your thoughts and feelings through your words and your actions. No matter what the people around you, or the media talking heads, are saying or doing, stick to your beliefs if they feel right to you.

PERSONAL STORY

I did an important 'THINK-FEEL' my Junior year of high school. All of a sudden, our media (magazines, news, movies and gossip city) were promoting 'going all the way', meaning having sexual intercourse. The pill was now very reliable and available and Roe vs Wade was about to pass. I felt weird about why it was *all of a sudden* ok and thinking, 'huh?' I *felt* making love was special. And I trusted that I wasn't an idiot. I knew it's how babies were made so…so who is saying just go ahead and do it?' I questioned it. Big Time. I had to ask myself – my inner self. Keep in mind, we didn't have the 24/7 media sex cycle you all are slammed with. But now something outside us (the media) was giving us the ok? *This struck me as odd.* It may have been when I first started trusting myself and not media's hype.

Listening to your heart and intuition is the tool that builds *character* and *integrity. You are learning and growing and developing a sense of self just by reading this book.* There is nothing more important. You'll be given lots of great self-worth creators in Chapter 12. This kind of inner growth will protect you in many life situations.

Right now, while in school, your number one goal is to learn and grow into a *cool and centered* being who is willing to get to know and love YOU first. You have heard this a lot. But how you love you is rarely shared. It's more than eating the right food (ha ha) and being kind to others. It takes gaining knowledge from books like this (Part 3 especially) and a willingness to identify and feel (no judging) the feeling. It also helps if you can find, share and listen to honest adults *you respect.* You deserve the utmost respect from others, *but first you must demand respect from yourself.* It is actually more important than grades! You are brave, and now wiser, for reading about readingabout tough subjects.

> Listening to your heart and intuition is the tool that builds character and integrity. You are learning and growing and developing a sense of self just by reading this book. Your number one goal is to learn and grow into a cool and centered being who is willing to get to know and love YOU first.

A Mantra for Self-Respect & Physical Intimacy

Say aloud three different ways! Go ahead...
Be dramatic.

Be assertive.

Be sweet.

"IF IT AIN'T LOVE . . . IT AIN'T HAPPENING!"

"IF IT AIN'T LOVE . . . IT AIN'T HAPPENING!"

"IF IT AIN'T LOVE . . . IT AIN'T HAPPENING!"

Now add...

"All in its perfect and right time."

C H A P T E R   9

I DID HER

How Guys Really Think, Flirting, and Waiting

A STORY TALE

The Computer Enters Homeland

Once upon a time Kyle, who was in middle school, went to Chad's home to see his new computer. It was the late 90s, and Americans were just beginning to put a family computer in their homes. Kids wanted to play video games, and parents wanted to play with photographs and send emails.

The two seventh-grade boys were playing on the new desktop computer that had been placed in Chad's bedroom. This was before laptops and back when the internet was still very new. Kyle knew his parents would not allow him to have a computer in his bedroom. But Chad was an only child and seemed a wee bit spoiled. He got almost everything he wanted.

Kyle's mother came by to pick him up. Chad's mother let her in and walked her back to Chad's bedroom. Having heard that the internet was not *parental-guidance* friendly, Kyle's mom thought, *no computer is going in our kids' bedrooms.* Keep in mind this was when computers first came into the home. Parents were determined to oversee and guide what their children could be exposed to.

As the boys played on the keyboard, the moms watched for just a minute. Out of nowhere a cute little blonde girl's image popped up on the computer screen. She was a Mouseketeer on the Nickelodeon channel. Both boys surprised their moms by blurting out "ho" at the same time. The word "ho" was still a fairly new pop culture word. It had entered the pop culture lexicon through music videos and songs that radio stations would not allow. The boys' message was clear: neither had a high opinion of this Nickelodeon teen queen.

Kyle's Mom asked, "What? What is wrong with her?" She glanced over at Chad's mother with a perplexed look on her face. This was before the Nick star became a female rock idol on MTV, dressed like a private schoolgirl, sporting braids and a short plaid skirt. And before her infamous snake video. It was Britney Spears.

What in the heck are these kids seeing that I'm not? thought Kyle's mom. On the way home, she asked him to explain why he had called this young teen TV star a "ho." Kyle had no real answer. He had no words. He simply didn't seem to think much of her.

What was clear is that both boys knew what they liked, and what they did not. It was as if they had seen this young teen's future before it actually happened.

THE END

RAISING THE BAR & MORE CSGs

What does *raising the bar* mean to you? Think of a diamond. A lump of coal isn't transformed into something beautiful just overnight. It takes time to *become* a diamond. Adolescence is the beginning of learning how to observe, play, flirt, and practice communicating one-on-one with a guy.

You are best served by taking lots of time practicing how to do this. It would help to know a few "boy basics," like how guys think (in general) and how to share with them. What will help you a whole lot is remembering that in all situations (friendship or romantic), it's the girl's job to call the shots when flirting, or just talking with a guy. This *"girl's in charge"* mentality is for both the girl and the guy's benefit, and adolescence is THE time to practice. Remember, the word "adolescence" itself means "to grow into maturity."

> Adolescence is the beginning of learning how to observe, play, flirt, and practice communicating one-on-one with a guy.

What really helps here is to remember the **CSG's** (Common-Sense Generalizations) I shared with you in the first chapter. These can assist you big time when practicing communication, learning to flirt, and creating boundaries. Let's review a few of them again:

- Number One: guys do not like sleazy girls.
- Number Two: guys do not like easy girls- for more than a night or two.
- Number Three: guys do like flirting, kissing, and one-on-one communication.
- Number Four: guys do like the idea of *love and affection,* but it's not a young male's first go to the way it is for a girl.

The male hormones do not always make guys the sharpest communicators. They need your help in learning to play along, and to play *respectfully.* This may sound politically biased. It also happens to be true. At the risk of stepping on some toes or sharing a few things your parent may or may not agree with (perfectly OK . . . just ask them if they agree or not and to share their ideas of *why or why not*). Here are a few more:

- Guys don't fall in love with someone cheap.
- Guys fall in love with a girl they respect.
- Smart chicks are a turn on—though some guys act like we aren't.

> The male hormones do not always make guys the sharpest communicators. They need your help in learning to play along, and to play respectfully.

- Most boys *like* the challenge.
- Many boys do brag about breaking a girl's Standards & Boundaries
- Respecting yourself and knowing your Values is a turn-on for guys.
- Guys are intrigued by girls that have other interests: sports, creative arts, design etc.

THINK & KNOW - FLIRT & GROW TIME

"But the guy wants me to . . ." Wah waah waah. Nope. Make a tricky situation into a *think-and-grow-flirt-and-know* time. And yes, it is fun, especially when you know ahead of time that being sexually intimate is not on your playlist. Just **raise the bar**. Flirting is the bomb!

> Make a tricky situation into a think-and-grow-flirt-and-know time. And yes, it is fun, especially when you know ahead of time that being sexually intimate is not on your playlist.

If all this practice wasn't one of the *very best* (as in F-U-N) *parts* of growing up, I would not have bothered to write this book! Communicating and practicing a confident attitude while learning to flirt is the bomb! This is when remembering certain CSGs help you.

> Communicating and practicing a confident attitude while learning to flirt is the bomb! This is why remembering certain CSGs are so important.

It is important for you to remember all that your friend misses out on when she chooses to become sexually active. Growing a *real* relationship takes time. You need time to practice communication skills, and to recognize feelings while giving true respect and emotional connection a chance. Not having a guy's respect is how you get really hurt. There is *no need* to be super physical. Flirting and being romantic is a blast, and way more fun than *having s-e-x*. Hear that?! IT FEELS WAY BETTER and YOU DON'T MISS OUT ON ANYTHING BY WAITING, Except . . .

1. Fear of disease,
2. Feelings of having been used
3. Being ignored or talked about
4. Going to the gynecologist to receive contraceptives
5. Ditching your girlfriends because he becomes your focus

> Not having a guy's respect is how you get hurt. There is no need to be super physical. Flirting and being romantic is a blast, and way more fun than *having s e x*.

6. Fear of a possible pregnancy...and finally,

7. Having to see him at school for the next couple of years and being shunned- another scene that never quite goes away.

Waiting is *raising the bar* and replacing self-loathing with self-assuredness. It makes life easier and *more special* when you fall in love with the right guy and the right time is placed before you.

When you make the decision to take time to communicate, flirt, and play along romantically, you will naturally experience feelings of self-worth and find out you are being cared about just for being you. More important, you are developing an amazing sense of self and communication skills. A worthy guy will bend over backward for you and be much more attentive when there is no heavy sexual involvement. Why? Because he'll start to get that you are not one to lower your standards (i.e. like chasing him) and he'll begin to realize he needs to value you as much as you value yourself.

The Number One Thing to remember from this chapter is this (and don't bother me with political correctness. We don't *think* like guys): Guys *want what they can't have*. But that's perfect! Why? Because not only do you get to set a comfortable pace of getting to know each other, you can help guide him in communicating with you in a real way. Before you kiss a guy...find out who he is by...

> We don't think like guys): Guys want what they can't have. But that's perfect! You get to set a comfortable pace of getting to know each other, you can help guide him in communicating with you in a real way.

- Talking to him *one-on-one* and *on the phone* at night. (a fun practice)
- Tell him he must talk to you on the phone or he's history.
- Be flirty,and a little mysterious with your voice- and zero face timing.
- Do not to call him. This is a no-no. Sorry, but it's chasing.
- Do not call him your boyfriend until you hold hands and get to know him as a person.

Try this. *Instead of kissing the guy at the party, look into his eyes, tap the end of his nose with your finger, and then sweetly say, "Call me some time," and walk off. You are sure to make a lasting first impression! And you are in control . . . as you should be. Talk about confidence!*

Did you know talking, holding hands and kissing is sexual and can be an act of emotional intimacy? And it's all good and glorious. Its intelligent flirting.

Heavy sexual activity at a young age often damages a girl emotionally and it's not necessary. Did you know talking, holding hands and kissing is sexual and an act of emotional intimacy? And it's all good and glorious. It's intelligent flirting.

Your self-esteem and feelings of self-worth can be easily taken down. How and Why?

Your world, your social life, and the situations you experience at school change from day to day . . . and *he* changes too. Heck, he's a growing teen guy! Your body may develop early, but your mind, heart, social intellect and Spirit are not ready for an adult experience. The above techniques are communication tools that can work for you, if you use them.

You will get there eventually. Rushing anything is asking for heart break. Ha! The Bachelor is a great example. **The desire to be loved** and/or **fit** in is strong. But I promise, you *can* receive those exact feelings with a boyfriend you are not sexually intimate with! Yes. Some girls want to go ahead and *have sex*... just so they can say that they have *"done it."* This doesn't make them stronger or smarter. Physical intimacy before you are ready shortchanges you and can diminish your growing self-concept. Many females in their mid-to late twenties today are realizing what they unknowingly allowed to be taken from them; something they can't ever get back.

> I promise, you can receive those exact feelings with a boyfriend you are not sexually intimate with!

A CAUTIONARY TALE

The Mom Who Hadn't A Clue

Once upon a time (in 2008) Cassie, a senior in high school believed she needed to lose her virginity. She felt she was different for still not having '*had sex*.' (Therein lay her problem—or one of them anyway).

Cassie's mother had rarely talked with her about relationship, romance, and love. Like many parents, they shared only a few facts about s-e-x. And nothing about the in-between stuff. Her mother had received no information from her mother (way more common than you would think) Cassie's grandmother. Despite this mother having her doctorate in humanities, she as unaware of the **Five Biggies**: Communication, Relationship, Trust, Romance and Love. How to value herself sexually was not on her radar. The mother had little information, nor did she have any positive experiences she could draw from. And though information from a trusted source could have helped the *mom share* with her daughter, it just never happened.

The mother, who was not particularly faith based, made a poor decision. During Christmas break she decided to take her daughter on a cruise. Nothing wrong with this in itself. However, she thought it a fine idea to take her daughter on the cruise to . . . lose her virginity!

What the . . .?! Cassie was not clued into having this special human experience with someone she loved and respected and who loved and respected her. Now in her early thirties, she has a great job she is good at, but she is still clueless when it comes to relationships. She still wonders where she can find a love that she can treasure and who will treasure her.

THE END

P. S. And yes, my mouth dropped hearing it.

What this senior in high school lost was not just her virginity. The young man she found to engage in this sexual physical act was probably happy to accommodate her. Heck, maybe he was a virgin, or just happy to *get some*—as they say... when s-e-x happens but isn't *honored.*

Q & A DIALOGUE TIME

1. How do you think Cassie felt after going through with her plan?
2. How do you think she'll remember her first time?
3. Do you believe this is a memory she will carry for the rest of her life?

Instead of getting caught up in the complications of sexual activity, along with the weird sadness that never fails to show up afterwards, enjoy your adolescence! Don't tell anyone this . . . but you have the rest of your life to engage in meaningful adult activities. Till then, rock it steady! You have only one time in life to be a teen.

Life is truly your oyster when you stay conscious,
and remember to love you, first.

**Some times you
have to show them
how!**

C H A P T E R   1 0

MAKING OUT IS MORE FUN
PART 1
COMMUNICATION
AND INTIMACY

Romance, flirting and affection are the biggest
highs of a good life. Making out is not only more
fun, it helps develop your innate girl power. It's a
great practice in intimacy and communication.

"Let's focus on communication.", "I don't
want to fall in love off of sub tweets." "Things
work out better when you plan it." & "I just
need the time . . ."

Lyrics by 18-year-old Khalid

A young male singer had these lyrics in his new song. He is a
guy who knows what he wants. Naturally he is thinking like
a guy. And yes, at the end of the video it shows more of what
he is thinking (and wanting). He hopes he will head straight
to a bedroom with his newest interest. Enter the cool chick
with substance and style. By this I mean a young female with
relevant info, great logic, and who knows her boundaries. She

knows to encourage real communication. She sits him down in a quiet area of a room, and says out of curiosity, "Tell me what's going on with you. I'm interested."

Don't tell anyone . . . but she just rocked his world.

Because we live in a time where many humans are taking directions from media, honest *heart-to-heart* connection and authentic communication are rarely seen or honored on screen. Consequently, they are not often experienced or practiced in real life There is an old saying that warns us to be aware of *cheap thrills.*

> Because we live in a time where many humans are taking directions from media, honest heart-to-heart connection and authentic communication are rarely seen or honored on screen.

Sexual activity shown or sung about in detail
is a large bag of cheap thrills.

As I oversee the final edit, one of *the* largest movie producers in the world just got axed. He stands accused by many of being a sexual predator. Thirty years of trying to force young women to satisfy him; he is going down. He is one of the many culprits in today's media who have lowered the values of our culture.

In 1989, a strange (at the time) movie and movie title came out. *Sex Lies and Videotapes with Director Stephen Soderbergh was a first.* I remember walking out of the theater *feeling like something did not seem right.* This movie won an award for its shock value. It was another first to help lower America's norms and values. Eventually such movies became the norm.

Are you able to see how we all get played? People young and old today are often traumatized by what has been allowed to creep into the public these last 30 years. Like a respected public servant said recently, "We are all just wanting things to go back to the norms and values we knew." And he was not a religious right guy.

You and the generation before you can't help but be confused about what sex and love are and how beautifully they go together, *naturally*. Guys wonder why they can't find the right girl. And too many girls fail to connect the dots by not knowing their Values, Boundaries, and Standards. A crude but funny thirty-year-old is a perfect example—or should I say *victim*—of trying to "have sex" and then wondering (like many others around her age) why it isn't happening. She makes really crude jokes about being sexually active (like it's turning on a faucet) and receives millions of dollars. She is boo-hooing with an entire generation of young adults who are wondering the same thing.

Media has portrayed sex as something you just *do* and then *get*. Well . . . technically that's what it is. But concerning human intimacy and lovemaking, nothing could be further from the truth. And many young people are missing out. Emotional intimacy is something you discover, nurture, and receive. It's an art: The Art of Romance. And it all begins back in middle school where a boy and girl learn to communicate one-on-one, slowly, thoughtfully, and with respect.

One-on-one verbal communication, flirting, affection, and romance are the silver lining of a life being lived well. But it starts with communicating one-on-one and becoming comfortable with each other. You will remember kissing and making out forever and be happy to share about it, long after you're married, even when your an eighty-year-old! Reflecting on blatant sexual activity? No way. The thrilling details of meeting, sharing and kissing all come back with feeling... when *that* song plays decades later!

JOURNAL TIME

A Fun Quiz

1. List three songs you think are romantic, but not sexual.
2. List three movies that light you up, and that you consider romantic.
3. Write one or two paragraphs that describe a romantic situation.

List three songs you think are romantic, but not sexual. List three movies that light you up, and that you consider romantic. Write one or two paragraphs that describe a romantic situation.

Bonus reflection question:

4. Are you able yet to connect the dots, see *how and why* we all have gotten tricked?

This is what secondary school is about: taking the time to practice communicating, learning to trust and sensing the bigger picture of life.

You will benefit greatly by beginning your quest for healthy communication, great relationships, and perhaps romance by becoming familiar with certain books, romantic movies, and awesome love-based music. Flirting and showing affection will become more natural once you start communicating with a boy you find attractive.

Talking and/or flirting with a cute guy in a room full of people is a fun form of communication. Put away the phone. Keeping your phone off and out of sight will allow you to *experience* authentic, one-on-one interaction. Looking into someone's eyes is often the beginning of truly getting to know someone. This practice helps build your communication skills and get comfortable, helping build confidence—both yours *and his.*

Please keep in mind what I shared in Chapter 4: new research has found an under-developed frontal cortex in the brain of one third of 19- to 25-year-old males. Here's my take on this: it may not be just from constant screen activity, but from a lack of real communication. *Talking* on the phone counts *as* real . . . live . . .communication with you girl!

KEEPING YOUR POWER & GROWING YOUR KNOWING

Being sexual while still in school often keeps a girl from knowing what she really likes and clueless on how to form a relationship based on *trust and respect.* Having sexual relations when you are young (still in school) too often keeps you from engaging in the fun practice of getting to know the guy.

Adolescence is *the* time to meet and experience a wide variety of people. I remember watching a couple of my friends in school who seemed to fade away. They quit thinking or caring about what was important to them. Some girls began to live for the guy, and even forget their girlfriends. Remember this, when a girl turns her body over to a guy, life automatically gets more complicated. Being overly sexually stimulated and engaging in s e x can easily throw a girl's focus off from important developmental adolescent life experiences. You are here on earth to grow in many areas: communication, the arts (music, theater/film, design), perhaps sports and, yes, academics. Heavy sexual relations are not on that list.

Adolescence is *so* not wasted time. Though I know some days feel like it is. Every friendship that gets weird on you, every grounding (and I got a lot of those), every guy you thought you might like and turns around and acts indifferent, is a valuable lesson! Remind yourself of this. You will wise up, one *seeming* screw up or rejection at a time. I love the saying; your rejection is God's protection.

You will come to know

- What *you* love
- What makes you happy
- What not to do the next time
- What creative talents you have
- Not feel super guilty about having gone too far

> I love the saying; your rejection is God's protection. You will be come to know What you love What makes you happy, What not to do the next time, What creative talents you have Not feel super guilty about having gone too far.

A few times when I felt rejected, I would make stuff, like cool tops and dresses. I didn't have to run out and find some guy to be with. Always relying on friends is not a good setup or even logical. Instead, I would sew my brains out and show up at school the next Monday with something really cool on that I created. This in itself is a form of communication. I was learning to communicate and love the person I was to take care of and would always be with . . . me. ☺

IT'S A PRACTICE

Adolescence is THE TIME to practice branching out with your personality, focus on your likes, and meet a few worthy friends. You don't really need a gang. Also, communicating with a guy as a friend can be awesome. Not every cute guy has to be your boyfriend! I wish I had known this at age fourteen. **Group socializing** does give you time to practice basic communication skills and/or light flirting skills if you find a guy attractive. I have heard guys say when girls come on to them too strong, it's often a turn-off. They didn't want to go there! It truly freaks many guys out. These are the guys with great hearts, probably wondering, *what's going on with this chick?*

I am not referring to the guys you see in trash movies that do kinky sexual things at a party. Try not to encourage disrespectful *guy* behavior. Instead of showing him too much leg and skin, why not show him your confidence, kindness and personality? Ask him a tricky question. Give him time to think and show his knowledge. You both are developing in the personality department. Just have fun flirting and communicating.

Thinking back on those days, my absolute passion for fashion and for learning to create beautiful clothing... and my mom's info on guys saved me.

I wish I had had more boys as friends. This would have been great. This is something I believe your generation may be doing . . . and doing well. It is important to know your Values and Boundaries when having guy friends. It makes friendships with both sexes easier. What if you made practicing the art of communication one of your projects? Find a willing guy (or two). Don't tell them you are practicing . . . just start talking. You will be helping them too. Try guiding yourself and the guy toward being real, honest, and unafraid to be just who you both are that day.

ROMANTIC INTIMACY

Romance is *a practice* and flirting and *clean* teasing is the most fun practice there is! It helps you create very specific boundaries and, in turn, grow a healthy sense of who you are becoming. A fun, flirty relationship is a blast, and can help you enjoy feelings of self-respect and sensing the awesomeness of just being *you* with the guy. Simply flirting and sharing is the beginning of you learning and owning *you.* It's the first step in the unique *dance of intimacy.*

> Romance is a practice and flirting and clean teasing is the most fun practice there is! It helps you create very specific boundaries and, in turn, grow a healthy sense of who you are becoming.

It is so important to experience this dance of emotional intimacy many times. Heavy sexual intimacy is not part of this practice. In fact, developing emotional intimacy first is the highest form of being and relating. Then, if physical attraction is there (by both parties) you will begin to trust what feels natural and right for you.

GUYS DO NEED YOUR HELP

Taking time to practice communicating one-on-one, or on the phone, is more intimate than a sex act. And guys are slow learners. Yes, they will need way more practice. It can be scary, but this is where you both begin to learn one of the most important aspects of a good relationship; the T word—*trust.* It is often scarier for males and why most guys go straight for the physical. Most guys have a hard time doing intimacy naturally.

Here's a little/big secret: many guys would love to share with a girl they trust, without the pressure of being sexual. A guy may often say that he can't do the real thing (emotional intimacy). The truth is girls are making a huge mistake when they allow or initiate a sexual act neither she or the guy are prepared for, emotionally or physically.

GIRLS * THE STANDARD-BEARERS OF OUR WORLD

Why don't girls insist that a guy take the time to learn important communication skills? Well, it's not all your fault. The *lonely-loser* texting practice is a culprit for sure and has you both communicating in a half ass way. Also, societal media messages have you buying into the betrayal trap of just "having sex." And man, does it feel bad later. Kids get tricked. Instead of practicing *one-on-one* emotional honesty and taking the time to develop emotional trust, two teens go straight to the physical. "But whyyyyyyy?" whines the little Valley girl.

1. The girl does not think enough of herself.
2. She has yet to identify her Values, Boundaries, and Standards.
3. She's bought in to the media's hype about "having sex."
4. She got tricked into thinking she needs to lose her virginity.
5. She did not adhere to her personal

> The lonely-loser texting practice is a culprit for sure and has you both communicating in a half ass way. Instead of practicing one-on-one emotional honesty and taking the time to develop emotional trust, two teens go straight to the physical.

boundaries by saying, "Want to get to know me? Please call me on the phone."

I didn't write this book to trick you or to lie to you. You want to keep your VBS as a guidance system to keep your self-worth and self-esteem from going down the tubes. Hey, the right time and the right love in your life will happen. *And you will feel great about it.*

Discover and practice your VBS (chapter 13) and I promise you will come to understand and feel the importance of standing your ground. Too many girls just do not know their own boundaries, or where they stand or why. It starts with knowing the importance of real communication and relationship. Or . . . as they say, "You will get dumped," and wake up one day thinking, knowing, and feeling you dumped on yourself.

Ouch.

THE INCREDIBLE LIE

What a relief to get...really get that our teen years are a unique time in life and that you do not benefit entertaining the idea that you need to "have sex." Identifying your VBS and knowing your self-esteem and self-worth are growing can only happen through you. No one but you can do this.

Why is communication and relationship practice so important? Well for starters, we females are the standard bearers of *excellence*. Females create the standards for a society by what we *say, do, and allow.* I don't care what religion you are being or not being raised in.

> What a relief to get... really get that our teen years are a unique time in life and that you do not benefit entertaining the idea that you need to "have sex."

So, you think society sets the standards? Well, who is society? It's the people. And guys? Well, until the end of time (or unless the guy has a sex change preference☺), young guys (and many older ones) will think first of satisfying their primal wants: sex, food, and money. Women raised *before* the "smut fest" got into full swing in the late '90s, know this on a deep level. Women are superior when it comes to setting standards! And all the little hoochie mamas you see running around? Well, they bought into the *incredible lie*. They are not using their superior parts: their heart, their mind and their unique Spirit.

Ready for Chapter 10, Part 2?

Please kindly warn your mom to just chill...and breathe.

Whatcha think? Class & Style?

PART 2
BOUNDARIES AND
TECHNIQUES

SO, WHAT IS NORMAL?

Because there is very little normal going on these days, it's up to you to be the adult in the room. Why? Because adults (and the media) are not being honest with you about the bummer feelings of thoughtless 'go for it' s-e-x. Yes, you will have to monitor what you read and hear until society gets its head out of its wazoo. By this I mean too many parents will not allow themselves to admit what you are being exposed to. It will take careful awareness (by you) to be able to recognize and honor your feelings. It's a two-step process. This is where you need to explore your own personal beliefs—discuss them and write them out.

Values, Boundaries and Standards come into play here! The day will come, I promise, when you will feel something very special about who you are. And it will have little to do with sexual activity. Does that sound weird? I hope not. For young women, feeling special and loved comes way before sex.

As I share this with you, I'm thinking of one of the media heartthrobs: Justin Bieber. Perhaps Shawn Mendes is more your thing. I don't care if you're twelve or sixteen: it's the *feeling* I am talking about. What has this got to do with heavy physical intimacy? Nothing. It's *the feeling* of love girls would do well to take time to experience over and over again. I'm talking about Crush City; one guy for a while, then another; all the while knowing sexual intimacy is not part of your romantic dance.

> It's the feeling of love girls would do well to take time to experience over and over again. I'm talking about Crush City; one guy for a while, then another; all the while knowing sexual intimacy is not part of your romantic dance.

At a certain point in life when you've become more developed socially, the time will come when a guy you're crazy about will be crazy about you. But until then, let the kissing begin! This is what you do not want to miss out on! Becoming sexual at an early age blows it. Great guys often do not fall for girls who "put out." Thank God you don't have to live a life that *imitates* "Celebrity Love Life for a Day." You are the real deal, and this is YOUR real life. You owe it to yourself to take care of it. Playing Blackjack with your body, heart, and Spirit should be beneath you.

Until you have graduated from high school, being romantic and playful is way better than being in a heavy physical relationship. You know why? It just *feels* better. And this is one of TWO SECRETS boys and media does not want girls to know. They have actresses playing horny teens . . . ALL FOR HORNY TEEN BOYS! That girl you see on the sitcom that tells her parent she's ready to be sexually active . . . is a male screenwriter's fantasy.

IT'S A FACT

The same brainless scenarios are now repeated in many TV sitcoms shows us one thing. The sitcom writers have run out of good material. Girls from ages thirteen to eighteen or twenty or so, are way better off not engaging in heavy sexual activity. Being romantic and playful feels better overall than being sexually active . . . until a certain time in life.

*There recently was an exception to the crappy teen movies. Did you see the movie **The Edge of Seventeen,** where she was goofing around with the guy in the pool? She wanted to get to know him and have some laughs. And being a guy . . . naturally, he wanted more. Sex hormones run the male.* ☺

A female is meant to *grow into* a relationship with love and commitment. And guide the guy, if need be. This is Mother Nature's way. What's the upside? A lot.

> A female is meant to grow into a relationship with love and commitment. And guide the guy, if need be. This is Mother Nature's way.

1. Guys respect you— and real love has a chance.

2. You learn to build communication and emotional intimacy skills.

3. You grow unique respect for yourself for him.

4. Waiting builds confidence and character in you that no one can take away.

5. A guy is more likely to fall for you when the above happens.

6. Guys just don't like girls who are easy.

7. Sexual relations are awkward and disappointing without love.

8. The BIG THREE—pregnancy, disease, and self-loathing, are nonexistent.

THE TRUTH ABOUT SEXUAL INTERCOURSE

Some of you reading this may know what I am getting ready to share. I am sorry you found out the hard way. But know this: it's never too late to rethink and do something different from here on out. You have this right and this power! If all moms had grown up really knowing this stuff, this book would not be necessary. But most moms did not have moms that shared anything with them. Sadly today, it may be worse.

> It's never too late to rethink and do something different from here on out. You have this right and this power!

Do you want to be truly cared for and loved? This may be the only question you need to know the answer to. You can choose how you want to be loved in this life. Is feeling pressured to be physical what you really want? Guess what? Young women in their twenties and thirties are not all that wise about intimacy, love and sexuality these days. They too were raised in a male-focused hypersexualized media (teen sex movies) and no one told them anything except,

"Use a condom" "Get on the pill" & or "Get the HPV Vaccine". I often hear young women confess, "I just let it happen," or "I wanted to lose my virginity and now I regret it. Love was not around anywhere." There are ways to love yourself first. **Part 3** will show you how.

WANT TO KNOW A SECRET?

First, the act of sexual intercourse is almost always (like 98.9%) a big or little letdown for a girl. *It feels weird and it hurts.* This is a real shocker to a young female in the beginning. You want to put your hands on your hips and say, "What the heck? That hurt, and it wasn't really fun." Yep. It takes time and practice to enjoy something that is meant to be special and sacred. But then like real communication, real lovemaking takes time. *You almost feel kind of dumb for not having known.*

> It takes time and practice to enjoy something that is meant to be special and sacred. But then like real communication, real lovemaking takes time. You almost feel kind of dumb for not having known.

But girls don't always tell the truth about their first, second or third time. The likelihood is that the girl just *had sex* because she wanted to be liked, was curious, or she let the guy talk her into it. Or the worst: he did not really like her—*super ouch.* This hurts a lot and the pain is one's heart and psyche can last for decades.

"I feel dumb and used," a girl often says. This feeling lasts too long and goes into her psychological memory bank. Dang! Then low self-esteem waltzes in to her psyche. Even if the guy does not label her a "ho" or "easy" she may subconsciously label herself this horrible term.

So, she feels disappointed afterward. The guy may be happy but dismissive, or he may be truly grateful. But more times than not, the girl still feels like she got tricked, especially if love was not in the hearts and minds of both young people. Guys are not always thoughtless but can be with the snap of a finger. You must put yourself at the top of your love list. You can turn it around by becoming determined to work on loving yourself. Begin by taking the time to know your feelings, (meaning writing them down) and taking the time to finding your VBS. Part 3 shows you how.

THE EXCEPTION TO EVERY RULE

There are those over-the-top-in-love teens who just have to have each other because "It really is love" and "We will we be together till . . ." I remember a couple like that. Every school has at least one. The girl was a junior; she looked twenty-one. She was gorgeous. The guy was a senior. He looked twenty-five! They exuded sexual energy. She did get pregnant; they did get married. They were together for thirty-two years. They had two gorgeous children. They are now divorced. But you know what? In all that time she spent focused on her love mate (two years of high school), where was her social life? What happened to college or tech school? He was a great truck driver (true story) and a good father; she a good mother and a wonderful oil painter—an artist today.

But news flash! Life does not end after your senior year. It is just beginning. At the risk of repeating myself, you do have a choice—lots of them actually.

THE VERY ART OF ROMANCE

I don't want to brag . . . but I was a queen of it. And mainly because I knew and was committed to my physical boundaries. It totally helped that my generation had *the coolest* romantic soft rock songs ever created (check out the list, and just listen.) You won't think they're dumb. You will most likely dig them. But what also helped is most girls knew it was OK to *just kiss and fool around,* meaning *nada* below the belt-even if it was someone you really liked and he liked you. ***

Being romantic with a guy you think is cute is a great way to learn more about you and him. Here are some ways to be romantic:

- **The Glance**—demure and sweet. Just a bare turn of the head, and a sweet smile with brief eye contact.

- **Talking/Sharing**— How are you most comfortable? Girls are really better at starting a conversation . . . so do it!

> Here are some ways to be romantic:
> The Glance
> Talking/Sharing
> Eye Contact
> Holding Hands
> Kissing
> Making Out

Ask what his favorite movie is and why. Same goes for music. I talked, and still do . . . too dang much. But some guys love it; it lets them off the performance/carry-the-conversation hook. It's a fine balance. Flirting and romance is great practice and a lot of fun!

- **Eye Contact**—This practice is a lifelong skill practice. If you are brave, it can give you a sense of where a relationship might go. If a guy cannot make eye contact, kissing is NAO (not an option).

- **Holding Hands**—It's the very first physical connection. It is the first physically romantic and intimate action. A lot of guys are not tuned in to this. Like, how often do you see people holding hands these days? This is where you get to help him. Walking next to a guy can be thrilling and sweet. Wait. See if he grabs your hand. Girls are more aggressive these days. I wouldn't say grab his hand even if he is shy. But there are exceptions . . .

- **Kissing**—Like months before sexual intimacy! Helloooo . . .

- **Making Out** – Means longer, grubbier, hotter kisses and holding each other. Hands tend to go where they should not be . . . and yes, it's up to you to move them. ☺

Please be patient . . . if you already know this stuff. Kisses can be short and sweet in the beginning, later . . . long and drawn out if you really, really like the guy. The media has tried to trick us all sending messages like, "Ah, just skip it!" Yeah, right. Why? So, the producer, young writers, and actors don't have to develop the creative talent to write good intimate scenes. No, it's worse than that. *They make lots of money targeting horny young guys.* Give every female on the planet a break! These repeated scenes today have hurt millions of young females who have never been taught and did not practice what I am sharing in this book. Man did they miss out. ☹

TEACH HIM TO KISS

Play, practice and become an expert on romance! And there are many, many different ways to kiss - on the neck, on the forehead, the shoulder and on the lips. Kissing is an art in itself. It's so important to linger on kissing. You want to go slow and learn the give-and-take of this intimate act. Did you know that some boys have a hard time kissing? Emotional and physical intimacy is often foreign to them. They become sexual before they experience the intimacy of hugging and kissing! This is more common with boys who have been hurt by alcohol- or drug-addicted mothers. Guess what. When it comes to kissing and communicating, you're the teacher! Why?

- Because it's more fun.

- It feels great.
- It's safer physically.
- It's good for your self-esteem and his.
- Emotional & physical intimacy is a learned skill.
- It makes you wiser.

> When it comes to kissing and communicating, you're the teacher! Why? Because it's more fun. It feels great. It's safer physically. It's good for your self-esteem and his. Emotional & physical intimacy is a learned skill. It makes you wiser.

Warning: If the guy likes you but knows you have been sexually active with someone else, he may go out with you, but do not be surprised if he doesn't *fall* for you. But this is not something you need worry about. You get to call the shots.

TECHNICAL, PRACTICAL AND SAFE - Mentally and Physically

Let's get serious . . . and practical. As you get older, you will find it harder and harder to draw a clear line around physical intimacy; this is much easier to do while you are a younger teen, provided you know to take your time and know your Values, Boundaries, and Standards. I know it can be done. Loving yourself, first and foremost, is *the* priority. And building your self-concept while protecting your future love life and the family you may one day create.

> GAGE WHAT YOU ARE DOING/ ALLOWING BE CONSCIOUS! The easiest way to do this is to use the BBT.

GAGE WHAT YOU ARE DOING/ALLOWING
BE CONSCIOUS!
The easiest way to do this is to use the **BBT.**

THE BASEBALL TECHNIQUE/ THE **BBT**

FIRST BASE—Kissing, light hugging, heavy hugging not lying down . . . wait until your junior year . . . if at all possible.

SECOND BASE (age 16 ½ to 17 at least)—After many months of the above, and if you know this guy is yours for as long as you can be intelligent, loving and respectful, he may place his hand under your shirt. Drag this out. Enjoy it. Don't allow under your bra. Are you ready to accept that you will be seeing this guy in broad daylight with another girl when you are no longer a couple? Personally, I never wanted to experience this while in high school: seeing a guy I had been intimate with . . . and then poof! It's over. Not a good feeling—and it doesn't go away.

THIRD BASE – If his hands are below your belly button . . . if you let a guy touch you under all your clothes, at the entrance point of you-know-where . . . you're screwed. Sorry about that word. *Think about it.* Do you really want to see a guy at school, a party or—God forbid—in class, who has touched your most sacred space . . . on or in your body; meaning . . . the boy's hand is in your pants and his fingers are inside you, like where a baby comes out one day? Be *good and ready* to say, "No. Sorry, but this isn't okay with me." So... no hands below your waist in front, over or under your jeans. BELOW THE BELT is NAO (not an option).

If your boyfriend is totally worked up, be thoughtful and say, "You are welcome to go into the bathroom if you are getting too . . . uh . . . well, you know, worked up." Smile be firm, and move away from him to *allow him to go*. I always see the future; SO, SHOULD YOU.

Visualize this:

It's the following week. You're walking down the hall Monday afternoon. You're a bit nervous to see him. Where was he that morning? Then at 2 p.m. he sees you. His eyes dart past you as if he didn't see you (but he did), and last Friday night he . . . he what? His hands were on you where? Think he might like you more next Monday morning? Oh really? Who said so? And again . . . how would you FEEL . . . in broad daylight? This same scenario goes for any oral activity.

NAO. (not an option)

HOME RUN—He has entered you with his penis, which is technically called sexual intercourse. NAO (not an option).

TALK TIME

Please feel free to share your thoughts on the baseball theory with a respected and trusted source (Mom, aunt, responsible caring adult) or by going to www.YourBodyisaGift. com.

1. Had you heard of the baseball theory before reading this book?
2. Do you think you would use it? Why or why not?
3. Did you notice that oral copulation is not even a base? It was a porn thing ...until. ..

It may seem dumb, *but the BBT is a heart, health and self-esteem saver*. It keeps you conscious and from going too far. It is an excellent tool in a time in human history when many young women don't know self-restraint, or their VBS, and are looking for what is OK for them.

Bottom Line: The BBT is safe and effective. It helps remind you of what you are not ready nor willing to do and helps keep you aligned with physical boundaries. It is your job: to be aware of what you are doing physically. Never expect a guy to help you with this one! **Never**. If he does, it's a gift. Take it. Use the baseball technique for protective, self-affirming reasons, and to gauge yourself.

Allow the baseball technique to be your
mind-conscious stopwatch. *

Well, by now your parent is either freaking out or thinking . . . who knows what?

Just take care of you. If your parents are the type who feel powerless and are super afraid—they <u>may throw condoms at you, tell you to get on The Pill and have the vaccine</u>. Tell them to chill. I'm OK with the last one if need be. But never, *never* let them *assume for you* that you are going to be sexually active in high school!!! This is an injustice to you. Like you can't think for yourself. You will know when you know. Just make sure you are conscious. ☺

And just to cover my bases: if you're a senior and you are in a serious, loving and committed relationship . . . and it's almost graduation . . . well, welcome to responsible adulthood. I trust that you believe you and he are willing to handle the *potential consequences* that come with sexual intercourse. *Just don't act like it's no big deal.* Because...because IT IS. And please, both of you *-feel in your hearts-* that this relationship is the right committed relationship to become physically intimate—right *for you both.*

Phew . . . I'm glad this chapter is over. * Oops . . . Do I sound like your mom?

188

We do better
when know better

PART 3

YOU BEAUTIFUL YOU

Be willing to stop, ask & listen.
Life, God, ...our Universe
is always speaking to you

C H A P T E R   1 1

YOU ARE THE GIFT

Your Heart, Intuition, Mind & Spirit

*Taking care of your heart, mind and Spirit
will one day be your greatest job.*

I hope you have begun to grasp the important heart and Spirit connection to relationships and sexuality. Please, oh please be patient as I morph, again, into my mother and repeat certain concepts. The *Repeater from Repeats Ville* must return. Hey, it's only for your best, and the friend that skipped a few chapters. ☺

Your sexuality is connected to your heart, mind and body. And each are directly connected to your one-of-a-kind Spirit. This is inherent for most females from day one of life. Boys and young men are able to disconnect from this deeper part of themselves in ways females are not. It is up to you to get, really *get*, that sexual activity is naturally programmed in most females to be special, spiritual and loving.

> Your sexuality is connected to your heart, mind and body. And each are directly connected to your one-of-a-kind Spirit.

Let's go deeper. Some experts insist that the brain is the most powerful sexual tool. But this also applies to your creativity. Learning to observe what your mind is thinking and being able to honor your heart is the dance of life we are all here to learn. How you and your Spirit connect to your heart is for you to DISCOVER. It takes practice: a thinking/feeling practice connecting to yourself. By this I mean checking in with what you are physically thinking, feeling and doing. Some examples: *I am on the phone because* . . . (mind awareness), What are you feeling (heart awareness)? *I am feeling anxious. Hmm* . . . *I wonder why?* . . . (heart, mind and Spirit awareness). You may be feeling anxious, confused, sad, mad, or hurting. It is often more than one feeling.

Many adults might think you are not ready or able to learn this. They would be wrong. Adolescence is perfect! Just remember, this stuff takes time: time to practice and then time to sink in. One day, it will become like breathing. Please try not to wait until you're an adult. Why?

Most things worthwhile take time.

YOUR HEART

Nothing you do or say comes out of nowhere. If you take time to notice the connection between your body and your feelings, you discover your heart! The heart is often referred to as the first brain because it is often the first to get a message.

When we begin to honor our heart, we are ready to dig in and learn more about who we are. You are so much more than just a young girl soon to become a young woman. But few, if anyone is telling you this! And today's 24-7 media is doing its level best to have you think and feel like you are *just not enough*. The greater truth is that there is real power at the core of who you are. Your core is actually your Spirit which is connected to your heart, which is connected to your soul. (*Hey parents and educators, is spirit a word you are or are not comfortable with? Honest feedback appreciated. Go to* **Facebook YBG Parent/ Educator Group**)

The really good things in life often begin from *heartfelt* ideas. You will someday do wonderful things and be involved in exciting projects. It is to your great advantage to begin to honor the importance of your *heart, mind, Spirit, and body* connection. Why? For a God-zillion reasons. But let's start with what is fun and exciting. After all, this was the main reason for me writing this book.

Romance, love, and affection are the bomb. There is a space where the heart receives non-filtered good vibrations. If someone refuses to partake in affection and does not take time to experience romance, there is a blockage from the mind to the heart. They may be afraid to feel. This is important to be aware of when falling for a boy or becoming attracted to him. Can he connect to his more sensitive self, or is he jumping towards the physical? Awareness of another's actions is often connected to the heart.

Let your heart be your personal assistant. Doing this will help you tap into your God-given creative intelligence, creativity, and common sense. And the truth is, that sense of yours is *not simple common sense*. It is an *inner knowing*, super trustworthy and more directive than your heart. It is often referred to as *intuition*.

> Romance, love, and affection are the bomb. There is a space where the heart receives non-filtered good vibrations. If someone refuses to partake in affection and does not take time to experience romance, there is a blockage from the mind to the heart.

INTUITION ... A MAP & YOUR BEST FRIEND

Here's what I find really cool about being a girl. Females have *great intuition.* We develop intuition much sooner than most males. I mean, do you really think this loving force of Good/God/Universe would arrange for guys to give birth and raise children? I don't think so! This is not their fault. They are wired differently. Their hormones are full of testosterone. And many males (though not all) have been trained, "Don't cry, don't feel, don't connect to that place deep inside." This is starting to change, but slowly.

The personal power of connecting to your intuition you must never take lightly. Teens who become aware of this powerful connection start to feel great hope about their lives. You may already have come to accept much of this as true for you, or you might still be wrestling with these ideas. Through all this sharing, keep one thing in mind: no matter your past, going forward, BE THE EXCEPTION! Do your best to grasp this information, and maybe discuss it with a trusted source.

> The personal power of connecting to your intuition you must never take lightly. Teens who start to become aware of this powerful connection often come to feel great about their lives.

Intuition is an *inner knowing* that is connected to your heart and Spirit. What does it look and feel like? Well . . . I wish I could say that it is *just* a feeling. Though it can be just a feeling, it is much more.

I remember years ago, when I first read about intuition (in, of all things, a business book). I wanted to *experience* it. I sat very still and prayed to be shown intuition—or to somehow *feel* it. Though I hadn't a clue what I was doing, and no one told me, I wasn't too far off base. Something told me to just get *very still* and clear out the mind chatter. Well, who told me to do that? I just had this sense that I might receive intuition or a message if I just shut the @#$$&! up . . . and I did! It was like a slight whisper . . . a gentle direction. I will leave it to you to find your own intuitive ways. But as I write this, I realize it was my own intuition that told me to get still! It wasn't a voice, but a gentle whispering thought—a kind of feeling-knowing. Weird? In some parts of the world tuning in to intuition is part of everyday living. It often keeps people in indigenous countries safe from the unexpected.

> Your Spirit is yours alone. It is what makes you uniquely you. It is the essence of your innermost self. Your Spirit is what inspires your creativity and helps you love you.

I would love for you to tell me your thoughts. Have you experienced something similar? Think back . . . to that time you did something, not really knowing why, and it worked out great. Perhaps you stopped doing something that just didn't feel right.

* Please feel free to share it with me
At www.YourBodyisaGift.com click on 'Girls'

YOUR MIND

'So where does the human mind come in?' you may be wondering. The mystic Pashin ("mystic" means someone close to God) says our heart is the first to get us to feel. Oftentimes, our minds quickly take over by judging the feeling, and attaching a belief to that feeling. Yikes! Your mind can be good at directing you to think before acting, but the mind must be checked up on! *It is not always right.* Now

THIS I wish I had been told in my early teens. However, when you sense what you feel in your heart and practice a little "intuiting," you can enhance your knowing and gauge how much to trust your mind and its many thoughts.

If your mind is only half conscious from too much electronics, food, or drug and/or alcohol addiction, good luck! Any of the above can easily make Jack a dull boy and Jill a

goofy girl. Being an adolescent is hard enough. Why make what is going on in your life harder by blurring and distorting what may or may not even be happening? Have you ever gotten off your phone or computer and felt a little fogged out? That's what I'm talking about. The heart, mind, and intuition are almost asleep.

Please honor yourself. Your mind is here to serve you, but you must, at times, *direct it* from fearful and *less than* thoughts. Our minds can have us thinking things about people, places and things in ways that just do not match reality. Making a big deal of anything is you hurting yourself by adding your own spin on a situation. Do not let the little human mind boss you around. The human heart and Spirit are where your truth lies.

One great thing about living in the 21st century is that positive affirmations are now considered a daily Life Skill tool. Affirmations help us improve the quality of our daily lives and are a necessary tactic for the mind. Re-thinking and re-wording positive messages are gifts you create and give to yourself. ex. "New Day! New Way!'. In today's world we are mustto use better wording and think higher. Years ago, people laughed at the thought that we could actually *pivot* our minds. Oh, but we can! The Pivoting tool is the higher part of you taking charge and will be shared in **Chapter 15.**

YOUR SPIRIT – THE CORE OF HOPE & WHO YOU TRULY ARE

As a young female, you have many superior biological aspects. We have the ability, at a young age, to be aware of life on a deeper level. Dare I say spiritual? I knew this at 12 twelve years old; I could feel it. It was something I knew was mine and no one could take it away from me—no matter how many times I was grounded! Don't think you're weird if you feel it too. It's really pretty cool. As you get older, you will love this part of you, and be so thankful you can recognize and honor It. Your Spirit is yours alone. It is what makes you uniquely you. It is the essence of your innermost self. Your Spirit is what inspires your creativity and helps you love you. It is the part of you that *sees* and *feels* the adorableness of a puppy or feels amazed by watching a big wave or cool sunset. All of life is connected to you. Your one-of-a-kind Spirit helps you know this through intuition and your heart.

"So where is my Spirit and how might I connect to it?" Hey, glad you asked me. ☺ First, keep in mind the human Spirit is so deep and so meaningful that 90 percent of the population would rather watch TV or surf the internet than check into their own Spirit! I guess they are scared. No need to be. What I love about Spirit is the hope it feeds us.

Once you get brave and begin to identify and feel your feelings, you will indeed be on the road to believing you do, in fact, have all that I just shared . . . *right inside you.* Your willingness to write and do a few Life Skill tools will help you

199

come to know your Spirit. Both are personal action practices that help you *love you.*

ADD & ME

Last but *so* not the least . . . is **the practice of meditation.** Meditating is the number one Spirit-mind tool. Meditation is simple, but not always easy. There is a fun meditation technique I created in 2008: Listen Breathe Allow (LBA for short). I call it meditation for the ADD or highly creative soul. I happen to be blessed (ha . . . *sometimes*) with a highly creative mind. Professionals like to label it ADHD. I love how LBA *slows my mind down* . . . gently and lovingly. You will find this technique in Chapter 15, and on my website.

Your Spirit, though not visible, is what will naturally help you define and guide your Values, Boundaries, and Standards throughout your life.

A HEADS UP

It can be scary when you first begin doing the kind of exploration you will do in this next chapter. But it is soooo worth it. One definition of fear is *not looking;* most humans never do. But YOU... are ready. Deep down you know who you are.

Your **heart; mind & unique spirit** *are here now. They know what's up and will* help you to honestly identify your unique human characteristics. The following work ... is a major key to self- confidence. For me it was THE KEY. And I thought in high school it was my looks. Nope.

Persistence and doing the work has a fantastic way of helping us feel whole and worthy.

Learning what we value
often begins with our
parents. And yes that look is me
quesitioning Everything! Like
"Why am I here?"

CHAPTER 12

VALUES, BOUNDARIES, AND STANDARDS

Once you identify your Values and Standards,
your emotional and physical boundaries
are easier to create and uphold.

WHO ARE YOU?

What is it inside of you that might show others who you are, or have the potential to become? When we don't know much, it's easy to be swayed by a friend: a well-meaning guy friend, or a *not-so*-well-meaning girlfriend. Your values may be cloudy. You may not be aware you have any; but you do have them. As sure as you have a heart and Spirit. When we are unsure of what we value, feelings of self-doubt intensify, and we become vulnerable to persuasion from others. There is a way to *know* your values even as you grow and change.

> When we are unsure of what we value, feelings of self-doubt intensify, and we become vulnerable to persuasion from others.

IGNORANCE AND TRAGEDY

In the fall of 2016 three teen boys were charged with killing an innocent twenty-year-old male who was in the United States on scholarship from Australia. He was running down a road in a small mid-Western college town. The boys pulled up behind him in a car and shot him in the back. They told the Oklahoma police they had simply decided to go and kill someone that day.

Perhaps one or all three teen boys were raised by an overwhelmed single parent, or parents who rarely or never attended a faith-based center. This is often where boys learn beliefs about life, and what to honor and value. What if two of the three boys had attended a place of worship? Could one boy have that much influence over others? Hormones in teen boys are strong . . . but violence?

Many parents think a strong and sturdy value system could have prevented such a hideous crime. Oklahoma is part of the Bible Belt. I raised my boys in this area of our country. I will speculate and share with you that there is a good chance one, if not all three boys attended church growing up. Do you think that TV, violent video games, movies, and or the internet, influenced them? What if one boy had stood up and told the boy who instigated this hideous crime to take a hike?

Today's valueless media has had way too much power and has taken many of us on a less-than-admirable path. The slow and steady dive of Values and Boundaries in society and today's media has devalued human life and distorted a female's worth.

Television shows today often show an adult female as a power-hungry female politician or business woman. It then de-values her character by adding that she is a sexually explosive crazy woman. And fathers and single males complain that sitcoms portray them as the dumb and clueless. Viewers unconsciously adopt these stereotypes which disempower and devalue both sexes in the real world.

VALUES

Most of us start out by learning a set of Values and Standards from our parents. These values are often reinforced through attending a church, synagogue, or spiritual center (excluding extremist terrorist "religious" ones). Spirit-based organizations are a great place for building a foundation of values that honor all living things. Faith-based centers, even without a parent's influence, often introduce and reinforce the basic goodness of all humans, teaching respectful love, first for ourselves and then for others.

Over the past two decades, many adults in American society have questioned and even thrown out their parents' ways of worshipping and practices based around a *specific* religion. But few of us have a real desire to lower our personal values to what we are seeing today. Values of any kind have faded from everyday life.

Today's world is in some ways like the rebellious late '60s. But the Free Love liberation, by the year 2000, appears to have morphed into Sleaze liberation. What happened to the respectful middle ground? I believe this is something we are all good and ready to correct. And we must, if we are to live with authentic love and respect for ourselves and others. Don't tell anybody... but I think the guy in the White house is the wakeup call for our world. We all have a purpose. No one wants to live with zero boundaries or have an inability to respect others or our own core values. Chaos happens when leaders ignore or do not have core values. De-valuing other races, immigrants, and sexual differences creates human pain and cultural chaos.

Black Lives Matter was not created to make money, nor were Anti-Human Trafficking organizations created to cash in. Both nonprofits are devoted to stopping the devaluing of human beings and the degradation of minorities. These organizations give us hope for a better tomorrow. But it starts with each person knowing *what they value, having boundaries* and standing up for their values and beliefs. **Identifying your values** can be tricky. Real relationship, romance and love become hard when you don't know what or where your values are. You may love Hawaii but stepping into the Pacific Ocean while visiting Venice Beach and deciding to swim out "that a way," assures you of nothing. The same goes for a lack of values and deciding *what to do* or *how to be* in a relationship. Going *that away* can have you sinking instead of swimming during adolescence and continues into early adulthood.

> Black Lives Matter was not created to make money, nor were Anti-Human Trafficking organizations created to cash in. Both nonprofits are devoted to stopping the devaluing of human beings

> You may love Hawaii but stepping into the Pacific Ocean while visiting Venice Beach and deciding to swim out "that a way," assures you of nothing. The same goes for a lack of values and deciding what to do or how to be in a relationship. Going that away can have you sinking instead of swimming during adolescence and continues into early adulthood.

What I love about knowing your values is that it increases self-confidence. Your self-concept becomes stronger when you are not afraid to ask yourself what you really value. Your **VBS**

206

(Values, Boundaries, and Standards) is your inner guide when you are with others and in tricky situations. Tapping into your inner guide from the get-go helps all your relationships, both friendships and romances. Identifying your Values is an art, the art of living a good life.

Values help guide you to right action and making good decisions, even when you are unsure of something.

WHAT ARE VALUES?

Webster's Dictionary defines a value as something of "relative worth, utility, or importance, something (as a principle or quality) intrinsically valuable or desirable, to think that something or someone is important or useful."

People define values in different ways, which is why there is often a lack of clarity. Think of values in two ways: personal and group. Both are often stand-alone concepts that, looked at in a deeper way, show you to yourself!

Personal Values: A value is any concept, action, or thing (living or stationary) that gives well-being or higher purpose to human life or living life on earth.

Group Values are a set of worthy ideas, concepts, actions, living or stationary, that bring a sense of quality to a person, institution, or thing. Here are a few examples: honesty, integrity, accountability, respect and justice. They may also be your personal values.

And my favorite definition:

Value as a verb: to appreciate, cherish, prize, treasure, and love.

JOURNAL TIME

VALUES

A. Look up and write the definition (in your JOURNAL) of each of the words that appear below. Because we are looking at *value, and values,* as a human quality or principle, do not write a definition that concerns price and numerical estimates. Two requests (the learning curve is major here):

1. **If you can, use a book dictionary.** Physically flipping through the pages gives you introspective time to *think and feel* **the real meaning** of the word as it might pertain to *you.* (Side note: My 14-year-old editor did this one day in front of me. She picked up her iPhone and asked Siri the definition. ☹. Please grab a real dictionary if at all possible & take...your...time. NO rush.

2. **Please *hand write* each answer.** This gives your mind and *feelings* time to *connect* with your heart.

Allow yourself to *feel* each definition. It may not be comfortable. Just know you are *building up* your heart and Spirit, your own *inner knower (and best invisible friend!) and developing* a sense of *knowing yourself* in a deeper way: something you will not get from a new outfit or a new boyfriend. You may pleasantly surprise yourself!

Here's a Bonus: You don't even have to go to re-hab to learn this! Yippee. ***Write a definition for ...**

VALUES

MORALS

STANDARDS

PRINCIPLES

ETHICS

INTEGRITY

INTUITION

COMPASS

VIRTUE

IDEALS

HONORABLE

RESPECT

JUSTICE

CHERISH

TRUST

HONESTY

WISE

WISDOM

ESTEEM

RESPONSIBLE

CHARACTER

CLASS

STYLE

Please answer the following:

1. What do you value? (list ideas, things, subjects of interest)
2. Who do you value? (People you know or people you have not met is fine.)
3. What is the *quality* or specialness you cherish in the persons, things or animals you listed?
4. What might the Values or Standards be of the *people* you listed? Example: compassion, listening, understanding . . .

BOUNDARIES

Knowing your boundaries helps you grow a strong sense of self. I truly believe identifying them AND knowing why you have them is the key to a girl's self-esteem. When you are consciously aware that you have them, it not only keeps you safe, but it gives you a natural state of confidence in relationships. Boundaries can also help you big time in feeling safe from the actions or words of others.

There are two kinds of personal boundaries: *physical and emotional.* Many adults do not know their own boundaries with other people. Helpful social & sexual boundaries are not really taught growing up. An adult reminding you to *be*

> Helpful social & sexual boundaries are not really taught growing up. An adult reminding you to be aware of strangers and don't get in a car with one is not what I am talking about.

aware of strangers and *don't get in a car with one* is not what I am talking about.

WHAT ARE BOUNDARIES?

Definition of a boundary:
Something (such as a river, a fence, or imaginary line) that shows where you end, and another person begins;
A point or limit that indicates what should not be done;
Limits that define acceptable behavior.
Boundaries come in a few different shapes and sizes. There are *emotional and mental* boundaries, and there are *physical* boundaries. A boundary has the wonderful (but often hidden) job of keeping your *Inner Knower* turned on.

MENTAL & EMOTIONAL BOUNDARIES

Mental and emotional boundaries tell you when to turn away from what can hurt your heart and self-esteem. Here is an example:
Let's say you shared with someone one- on -one the following...
"I really like Tera's skirt," or something more personal like,
"I'm not sure about _____. I don't understand how to _____ and it makes me feel stupid."
You then notice (or feel) the other person ignoring you, or perhaps she rolled her eyes when you shared. Your second statement is shared from the heart. You were simply being open and honest. This is where knowing your Boundaries comes in. Some friends are great at knowing how to honor your feelings, and some may never be.
We are all raised differently. Some friends do not feel comfortable (or know how) to share from their heart. It's not

that so-and-so is a bad person. She may simply not have learned how to make a heart-and-feeling connection, or she might have yet to mature her communication skills enough to show compassion for you. It's perfectly OK to share from your heart. However, if the friend you have shared with says something hurtful *repeatedly*, it would be best to keep your emotional boundaries up. **You may or may not be aware** that you have this boundary-detector skill. This is why practicing real communication (vs. sexual activity) during adolescence is so important. And not to beat a dead horse, (chill equestrians - it's just a saying) but it takes *time and practice*. Adolescence and young adulthood are *the* time to begin to learn and practice how to express yourself and gauge who is safe. For example, ask yourself this: "Can I share from my heart with this person or share in a more general, from-the-head way?" Then use your intuition and feel for the answer. You can do this.

It's perfectly OK to share from your heart. However, if the friend you have shared with says something hurtful repeatedly, it would be best to keep your emotional boundaries up.

Adolescence and young adulthood are the time to begin to learn and practice how to express yourself and gauge who is safe.

I wish all teens were taught this intuitive skill.
There would be way less ridiculing and bullying in schools.

THE GIRLFRIEND DYNAMIC & SEXUAL ACTIVITY

A friend may be loving and understanding of your feelings, but not connected to her own heart and valuing her own body and feelings. I had a dear friend like this. She was so sweet and lots of fun! She was also a victim of past sexual abuse, but I didn't know this then. I had just thought she was loose with guys.

Check this. Back in the '70s and '80s most teens were not clued in to sexual abuse. We didn't think it was s-e-x when we heard about a young person with an adult who did something sexual to them. We simply thought the adult was sick and disgusting to even think of touching a young girl. Our reaction was natural (s-e-x had not yet saturated our culture). Hearing about a physical sexual act with an adult is a perfect example of what sex IS NOT.

> Back in the '70s and '80s most teens were not clued in to sexual abuse. We didn't think it was s-e-x when we heard about a young person with an adult who did something sexual to them. We simply thought the adult was sick and disgusting to even think of touching a young girl.

We knew this *instinctively* at 16. It wasn't cool, and it wasn't sex. It was *something else* . . . something that seemed *warped.*

> It wasn't cool, and it wasn't sex. It was something else . . . something that seemed warped.

But, teens (for hundreds of years!) did not have s-e-x thrown in their faces, training them to believe physical intimacy is . . . *"just sex" This* is where knowing your values comes in, regardless of what pervasive and invasive media throws your way. *Sex is never just* *sex.* Unless one is not thinking or feeling, or it's pornography. And that's half the problem.

ACTION BOUNDARIES

YOU must be responsible. Noticing then claiming that something is off when seeing certain movies pop up. Here is a perfect sneaky example:

I share this disturbing movie scene, so you get . . . really get . . . that only you can be responsible for calling out and turning off what you know in your heart is out of whack... should a weird movie or video clip pop up in your face. You do this to protect your heart, your spirit and your future love relationships.

Example:

A movie came out in 2017 that showed a 13-year-old girl being sexually active. The short description from the cable provider blew me away. (And I've seen a lot).

"A thirteen-year-old discovering her sexuality . . ." ***(yadda yadda)***

You do not need to discover your sexuality as a 13-year-old girl. (flirting & crushes do this naturally). Sexuality is meant to happen for girls slowly and naturally . . . unless some idiot director/producer or pornography creep ramps up his 'thinking like a guy' brain (but talking about a very young girl) and puts it out into the world. Girls don't naturally think like 13-year-old males! This barely teen girl has been influenced...by- *guess who.*

In this movie was a damaged 38-year-old veteran. The movie added in a 13-year-old boy who eagerly went along with the young girl, so desperate for love (emotionally abused by an overly strict father), so it would look *almost* normal. There was nothing normal about this movie.

When society puts this stuff out – it begins to normalize it. Guess who gets hurt? (Hint: it is not the pocketbook of the film company who made the unconscious decision to put this on screen and carelessly give warped messages to young teen girls.)

Just because you can do something,
doesn't mean you should.

Back to you. So, let's say you have a friend. She seems a bit . . . or flat out . . . clueless. She does thoughtless things with a guy, or even many guys. Perhaps her belief is that love can only come from *being sexual* with a boy. She gets all touchy-feely with a guy and . . . she may or may not leave her girlfriends in the dust. Big mistake. The guy often wants just the sex part. This is THE BIG FAT falsehood young girls and young women today are not being given helpful information about; <u>how very common it is to get dumped once you become sexually active.</u> <u>It is not discussed enough.</u> Older females need to share about this honestly. They often feel one or all 3 of the following: embarrassed, ashamed or guilty. They then push their screw ups out of their mind trying not to feel and say nothing.

A parent or a trusted adult must keep sharing the greater truth with you about young guys. A male's sex drive often has

When society puts this stuff out – it begins to normalize it. Guess who gets hurt? (Hint: it is not the pocketbook of the film company who made the unconscious decision to put this on screen and carelessly give warped messages to young teen girls.)

little (as in zero) to do with a "real relationship." Save your self-esteem, your friendship, and keep this fact in the forefront of your mind-

*Guys think sex. Girls think affection-relationship (a **CSG**) unless media has their way and gets girls to not think & act otherwise.*

Having boundaries is the key to self-esteem. And not having boundaries, both physical and mental, paves the road to low self-worth and a poor self-concept. Online is no different. A lot can happen with a few clicks on a keyboard. All the more important for you to define your online boundaries. Stay conscious and pivot away from certain people, certain social media groups, and websites. This takes PRACTICE, as in *thinking before responding.*

> Having boundaries is the key to self-esteem. And not having boundaries, both physical and mental, paves the road to low self-worth and a poor self-concept. Online is no different.

This boundary thing is SO IMPORTANT. Taking care of your heart, mind and Spirit is your greatest job here on earth. The best girlfriend you think is there for support is not always that aware. It is your responsibility to BE AWARE of any verbal and written abuse anywhere: in-person, on the internet or in a text. Awareness is the very beginning of creating your emotional boundaries. Emotional boundaries are super important because your sense of self is vulnerable to being damaged. Bottom line: YOU ARE IN CHARGE of pivoting. Just put your hand out and say to yourself or aloud **"No, no. No more."** Now turn on great music and dance to the power of having that boundary!

Yes! Turn on great music. Now, start dancing that feeling out!!

What Are Your Boundaries Today?

JOURNAL TIME

BOUNDARIES

A. Please *hand write* 4 **physical** and 4 **emotional** boundaries you have and/or some you want to have.
   Example –*Physical* *boundaries:* think electronics, alcohol, violent activity, boys moving too fast
   a. I don't keep electronics in my bedroom at night
   b. I don't kiss on a meet up.
   c. I might hold his hand on a first date but not kiss him.
   Example- Emotional boundaries with people - all people
   a. I don't laugh it off or just stand there when a so-called friend at school keeps talking down to me or slams me.
   b. I speak up if I hear someone makes a racist comment.

B. 1. Write 4 Physical Boundaries
   2. Write 4 Emotional Boundaries
   • Let's go deeper.

C. Write the 2 emotional boundaries you want to have today but have not yet established with...
   1. Friends
   2. School acquaintances
   3. A boy who likes you, but you're just not sure
   4. Teachers, coaches, tutors
   5. Adults- parent & others

D. Is there a specific boundary you need to work on I have not mentioned?

E. **Write a sentence or two** on each- on how you would feel more confident by knowing & remembering *you do* have boundaries -
   1. With friends
   2. With family members
   3. With a boy who is a friend
   4. Boundaries with a boyfriend

STANDARDS

Standards are weirdly simple, but important. As you take the time and do the work to find *your* Standards, you may realize Standards help guide, not just society, but your everyday life. They just make life easier.

Recently a mentor of mine (and Oprah's) said, "You must be the standard-bearer of excellence," and, "You are here to be a standard-bearer of existence." I *love* Standards. A kind of confidence happens when you actually define yours. Standards are a simple way to keep you in check.

I often see Standards in terms of *fashion and style*. Is that weird? It's probably because I was a stylist and designer for many years. Here's an example.

This beautiful woman comes to certain daytime community gatherings. She will sometimes show up wearing a tube top or

218

flimsy sundress. There are men in these meetings discussing serious topics. She is well-endowed, and it makes her stand out... and not for her creative input or beauty. Get what I mean? Before we look at the definition for standards and talk fashion, let's analyze the term "standard-bearer."

A *standard-bearer* **is a person** who is an outstanding leader, or who is representative of a group or movement. I see 18-year-old Emma Gonzalez from the Florida school shootings on February 14th, 2018, as a standard bearer of courage. She stood among many voicing her opinion loud and clear that "Adults are acting like children". It appears she has been brave in several areas of her life.

Today, many sane, honest, and well-meaning people in the United States agree that some of our world leaders are not worthy of serving as role models to a polite society. Although I am very comfortable with non-conformity, would it not be nice if more leaders had high qualitative value, were polite, and admired by others? Like I said in Chapter 1, some of our world leaders today act like they rose from the burial grounds of the Roman Empire and have come back to haunt us with low standards and valueless ways of being. Go figure.

Standards matter, because when we blow off standards we begin to see corruption in our society creep in. From sex scandals to mass killings; both hurt society and innocent people. Today lower standards are all in full swing. Humans having low standards influence others: they often scar and darken the human heart and spirit.

> Standards matter, because when we blow off standards we begin to see corruption in our society creep in. From sex scandals to mass killings; both hurt society and innocent people.

What Are Standards?

- **Let's keep it simple.** Here are some definitions:
- Acceptable but of not top quality.
- Normal, familiar
- A qualitative value—a criterion.
- A requirement of moral conduct: the model of a polite society.

Standards are personal and subjective. They have the power to harm or heighten person, group or culture's existence.

When I see a girl or young female dressed like her pimp helped her get ready to troll the streets . . . I want to scream. I get mad. But really (I'm talking feelings here) I go deeper and realize I am sad; sad that no one took the time to share with her how to dress like a million dollars—even with no money. But more important is what she loses out on when she dresses like a ho. Oops. Did I say that? Sorry. I just finished reading a book from a world-class editor. She said, "If you are a writer and you squelch your words, don't bother to publish your work." ☺ I love to learn, and I loved that.

SOME OF MY STANDARDS

I don't show bra straps. For me, it feels tacky and without style; as in the female didn't think enough of herself to find a racerback bra to wear. And Madonna is not my idol. But I love her music ☺

I brush my teeth before leaving the house.

I make my bed every day.

1. What are your Standards for the way you allow others to speak to you?
2. What are your Standards in speaking to others?
3. How do you usually treat those you don't really know but pass by?
4. When receiving change from a store clerk?
5. Please Add 2 standards you know you have to this list

B. Write out two standards you hold for yourself in how you talk . . .
6. To adults
7. Your friends
8. To siblings
9. To your parents
10. To your grandparents, aunts & uncles
11. To boys that are friends(explain)
12. To potential boyfriends
13. To your boyfriend (pretend you have one)

CONGRATULATIONS! YOU JUST DID WHAT MANY ADULTS HAVE YET TO DO! YOU DESERVE A GIFT! CAN YOU THINK OF ONE?

C H A P T E R   1 3

THE X-RATED G-WORD

"You are one of kind and needed in this world."
Michael Beckwith

A STORYTALE

Boy Meets Eagle

At age twelve and a half, my younger son spent two days and two nights alone up on mountain ledge in Idaho. When his father and I came to pick him up he seemed somehow different. He sat quietly in the back seat of the car we had rented. Then out of seemingly nowhere his head popped up and he blurted out, "I don't believe in the same God you do. I think God is in the sun and the sky and the trees and the birds."

He proceeded to tell his father and me about an eagle that had flown close by him, and how close he had felt to this life form. I opened my eyes really big, thinking, Whoa! What else did he experience out there in the wilderness all alone? I heard a deep conviction in his voice. This personal experience was his alone. And one he will likely treasure for the rest of his life.

The End

Highly evolved people such as Gandhi, Jesus, Buddha, Rumi, and Mother Teresa were each known to profess a very deep connection to a loving Source, sometimes called God, Creator, Universal Presence, or Mother nature. Many of us just use the G-word. I coined the phrase "The X-rated G-word" jokingly because of all the controversy schools, the media, political parties, and other organizations create when someone brings up anything *spiritual* or *religious*. I say, "Tough." Just what is so politically correct about pornography everywhere? "Deal with it, World!" This is my fifteen-year-old self still today screaming "Get a grip!" It's kind of like the weapons laws that make no sense. Darts are banned in public places, but AR-15 automatic rifles are OK. Huh?

THE G WORD

We have to talk about the G-word: God. "But whyyyyyyyy?" (whines the Valley girl.) Because your body is connected to your Spirit, which is connected to . . . God. Yes, your own loving God of all. What does this mean? It means everything. But first, some information that may help you these days. Today's societal chaos is not only becuase of the internet and sleazy media. Many families today are not attending a loving faith-based center.

In the United States, the Constitution demands the separation of church and state. Unfortunately, this has created another mess. Bringing up the G-word in public or government places has become unlawful. Today it can be forbidden for teachers to even whisper the

Bringing up the G-word in public or government places has become unlawful. Today it can be forbidden for teachers to even whisper the word Spirit or God in public schools.

224

word Spirit or God in public schools. But it's also one of many reasons nobody is SAYING ANYTHING that might help you understand sexuality and *how important it is concerning your entire being.* This disconnect is leaving most teens today unconscious (or clueless) of the deeper effects of blatant sexual activity. God forbid you should find out that your body is deeply connected to your heart and Spirit!

Many adults don't think you can get this as a teen. Then again, there are too many adults who today are not conscious enough to understand this connection for themselves. I believe many of them used to be more conscious, but life and media has worn them down. How many adults do you know who understand the connection between our sexuality and our spirit? And how many are willing to share about this connection in an honest, down to earth and loving way? I have met very few. It's not all their fault.

Gandhi and others like him were highly evolved humans who lived their lives very connected to their Spirit. Who knows what each of their sex lives were like. We almost automatically assume nonexistent. This may or may not have been the case. The reason their sex lives are not shared about in books is because *sex is special*, best to be kept private and created to be acted upon from a place of love and real relationship. And from one's Spirit. Helloooo!

Spirit, sexuality and love are tricky. Just "doing it" is a no-brainer. I recently shared this book's purpose with a twenty-four-year-old guy. He said, "It's bizarro! We see it

> Spirit, sexuality and love are tricky. Just "doing it" is a no-brainer. I recently shared this book's purpose with a twenty-four-year-old guy. He said, "It's bizarro! We see it and we do it, but nobody will really talk about it. You know . . . the way you are sharing with me right now."

and we do it, but nobody will really talk about it. You know . . . the way you are sharing with me right now."

Is it not weird that you can see visuals of sexual activity—even intercourse—on TV, on the internet and in movies; hear lots of sex talk about the action going on at school and in other places, but your school is not allowed to share with you a bigger, deeper picture? I wish it were as simple as Mom and Dad being afraid the school system might turn you into a Buddhist, a Christian, or a Taos sun worshipper. It is way more complicated. Consequently, you are not receiving the bigger picture, even when sex education *is* taught at school, *if* it is taught.

> You are not receiving the bigger picture, even when sex education is taught at school, if it is taught.

I may be going against the latest politically correct stance, but I will use the word "God" from here on out. People I respect often say "Universe," "Presence," "Source," or "Father-Mother God." You can choose whatever is *comfortable for you*. After all, it's *your* loving God of all.

WHO IS GOD . . . WHAT IS GOD?

God is big. I believe the correct word is "Infinite." God is Love. God is Beauty. God is Energy, God is the universal Presence of Good, all giving and all knowing. We can't possibly put God in a box or only one book. Oh, but how we humans try. This is important. Why? Because the sooner you begin to honor that your Spirit and a loving higher power of good exists *within you and is your life's essence*, the sweeter and easier life and tough decisions will be for you.

You could wait for adulthood before you give all this a try and continue banging your head against the wall trying to understand guys, parents and mean people. But the day will come when your Spirit will be your best friend, and life will get easier.

When I was twelve, I was aware that there might be something bigger than me—in me and on my side—and I don't mean my parents! I was lucky. I went to a church that showed me that God was, first of all, **Love**. And because of the Christ factor, I would always be forgiven. Yippee! As I got older and wiser, my God got bigger! Funny how that happens. Concerning churches, spiritual centers, mosques and synagogues . . . relax! Just listen and learn and give what is in front of you a chance. I realize now that my first eighteen years of life were meant not for just keeping myself from messing up, but also to observe and learn the basics of love—the good and the not so good.

About religion . . . don't sweat it. The basics of your Mom or Dad's belief system are usually a good thing, even a great thing. However, you may have parents who have become disillusioned with religion and are not teaching you anything about spirituality. That's OK, because now you get to choose how and where you learn about your Spirit and your loving God of all.

Have you ever attended a friend's spiritual hangout? Do give it a chance. Fewer families are attending church, synagogues, and mosques these days. And it does seem that this may be one reason the VALUES, MORALS, AND STANDARDS of modern day society are in the toilet. It's kind of sad, because all these spiritual centers teach love and the basics of good living.

Problems happen when well-meaning people who attend dogmatic religious centers feel they know the right way and look down on other people. This has divided us on just about everything, and it's one reason many parents today have backed away from attending a place of worship. The downside is many adults give up on, or postpone, finding their own Spirit. But darn, you deserve an informative Sunday school class, a fun Wednesday night Young Life meeting, a synagogue, a youth group, or spiritual center. Just find a way to go. Nothing need be set in stone.

MANY FAITHS, ONE GOD . . . A GOD OF LOVE

The bottom line: God is who God is to you. If you can't find God up in the sky (an many cannot), try visualizing God as this loving force of Universal Good who is always here for you. Hey, God may show up for you in nature. Many girls reading this are being raised in different faiths. I happen to live in small city right outside Los Angeles. Justin Bieber, the Kardashians and J-Lo all live five miles down the road. And they are all over the map! But that is *so* not the cool part. THIS IS!

> The bottom line: God is who God is to you. If you can't find God up in the sky (an many cannot), try visualizing God as this loving force of Universal Good who is always here for you.

I write in a library full of thirteen- to twenty-year-old's who are Asian, Middle Eastern, Caucasian, Hispanic and Black who have been raised in different faiths. Often young people do not think just like their parents. Heck, some of you may be mad at religion and at God (a lot of adults are). Perhaps you have been told you must "Love and obey or you will go to Hell," or "God is vengeful for those who don't . . . yadda yadda. I beg to differ! Here's excellent advice: make sure your Creator **is loving and forgiving**. What's that song . . . "Love is the Answer?" And this is Love with a capital L: a loving Presence that connects to your Spirit and soul is the ultimate goal when you're ready. Count yourself lucky if Mom and/or Dad have forced you to go to church, Synagogue or Spiritual Center. I have met many kids who have had no spiritual beliefs introduced to them whatsoever, and this can make life a bit tougher.

Society has changed a lot, and not all for the good. The community I live in has many families whose parents were raised in the Middle East. Their daughters are experiencing teen life very differently. Many religions tolerate little sexual showmanship . . . like ZERO! It can be severely strict. Young teens may find themselves in a dangerous family situation if they oppose their parents' belief system. Just STAY COOL, STAY SILENT and nod. **Practice loving** your own Spirit and don't confront. You may never see things as your parents do. And that's OK. What's not OK in many cases is acting out against their beliefs in any blatant way. You will be an adult soon enough. I give you my blessings during this difficult time of growing up.

No matter who says what about believing in God or not believing, all you need to know are the basics: God is Love. No one has a monopoly on The One. You have the right (if not now, some day) to go in a direction that feels right for you. Relax

> No matter who says what about believing in God or not believing, all you need to know are the basics: God is Love. No one has a monopoly on The One.

and feel confident in knowing you aren't in charge of every little thing, and you aren't alone.

Relax and feel confident in knowing you aren't in charge of every little thing, and you aren't alone.

Side note: You want to hear something weird and sad? If I were working for a certain university, a certain school district, or corporation . . . I could lose my job for writing this book! Nuts, sad, and totally not fair. Go figure. This tells you how important much of this information is.

listen breathe allow

Wonderful 3 word mantra
for slowing down your mind
as you meditate-

C H A P T E R   1 4

LISTEN BREATHE FEEL HEAL

"If you can feel it . . . you can heal it."

Learning the practice of observing what you feel is the key to helping you not react and go crazy. Ha! Most people avoid feelings simply because someone has not reminded them (over and over again) that feelings are just *feelings*. This does not mean they are not important. They are, in that they can be the direct connection to your *heart, mind, and Spirit*. But they do come and go. Learning to identify a feeling, and then letting the feeling go, is what this chapter is about.

Many young girls *avoid feelings* simply because someone has not told them that feelings are just *feelings*, messengers to help you. And feelings do come and go. Learning to recognize what you feel and having a tool or two that allows the feeling to go, is a *gift for life* practice. It's crucial to know what to do with your feelings. Why? Because they are connected to your heart, sometimes called "the first brain." When something happens to you, *your heart* is the first to get the message and then your brain.

Think of a feeling as a *sound alert* like when you hear your phone ring. You take notice. "Hey, my phone is ringing.' Your feelings are the message sender to your heart and…

mind. But like I said in the last chapter, your heart gets the message first. The mind (because of worldly and parental influence) too often interprets a feeling (other than happy) ... as something to fear. You start to believe the feeling is negative or bad...and you freak out or run away from the feeling. **Perfect example**: You eat a cheeseburger. You feel full. Your mind may twist it and you start thinking, *Oh . . . I am so fat.* No, you are full and most likely a little (or a lot) bloated! This, Dear One, is why I want you to have certain Life Skill tools: heart and mind writing practices to deal with what life throws your way.

SUCKY YUCKY FEELINGS

Please, please, love yourself enough to honor your feelings and know they are just feelings, and they pass. Rampant disrespect for our bodies happens when we are disconnected from our feelings. Sometimes feelings seem like they are just too much to handle. You can always gently say to your feelings, "Would you like to share?" It is important to remind yourself that your feelings are not facts. Being able to recognize a feeling is real personal power. Many adults today avoid them. That is why addiction is everywhere. **Many girls overeat**. It is often a way to stuff feelings. Or they eat to do just the opposite: they try and feel *something*. Many girls *feel* they are hungry. What they are feeling may be deep down and covered up as a result of years of not recognizing and

> Please, please, love yourself enough to honor your feelings and know they are just feelings, and they pass. Rampant disrespect for our bodies happens when we are disconnected from our feelings.

claiming what they really feel, *when* they feel it. Once you begin the practice of being honest in identifying your feelings, negative or false ones lose their power. One way to overcome and move though negative feelings is writing them down in your journal. It can also help to express them with someone who is safe enough to share with. But writing is still much more powerful.

Your ability to deal with weird, yucky, sucky, wish-I-didn't-feel-this-way feelings is power! You don't have to let the feeling take you out! Feelings are super intense in our teens. But there are cool ways to work through them. Your feelings are connected to not only your heart but even more important is the connection to your unique Spirit; the deepest part of you. When your feelings are not recognized or felt, a destructive urge to drink, drug, sext, cut, over-text, over shop, and over- or under-eat can develop.

> When your feelings are not recognized or felt, a destructive urge to drink, drug, sext, cut, over-text, over shop, and over- or under-eat can develop.

Eating disorders are very prevalent in today's world. They can develop from not knowing what you feel or what to do with what the feeling. A girl may rag on herself and think or say aloud, "Ugh, I'm so fat," or "I'm an idiot for eating all that ice cream." Simply catch yourself, recognize the feeling, then *until you have time to sit quietly and write,* call out the Mind Police! That voice is sometimes perfectionism, especially if you expect a lot from yourself.

> Simply catch yourself, recognize the feeling, then until you have time to sit quietly and write, call out the Mind Police!

235

Eating disorders are often built on the foundation of a harsh inner critic. But you don't have to allow that voice be mean to you. If it helps you to be guided in what you're writing, my friend (a young woman in full recovery from bulimia nervosa) wrote a book that can help any girl discover her perfectionism stories. Megan Reilly has written a personal book intitled **Escaping Perfectionism**: *Rewrite Your Story and Reclaim Your Life*. It has a quiz to find out which parts of your life are hurt by perfectionism, so that you can heal yourself. You can find it on Amazon.

Please be very aware (conscious) that you absolutely do have the power to choose to stop negative talk. You can pivot from endlessly repeating itself in your mind. It is a challenging practice for sure; a conscious practice where you catch yourself saying things you would never say to someone else. I sometimes call it *looping*. This simple decision, and then action (like not reaching for food or the phone- unless *you are looking for a sweet mantra* to replace the crappy thinking) will help with looping negative self-talk; telling us we are something we are not.

Absolutely do have the power to choose to stop negative talk. You can pivot from endlessly repeating itself in your mind.

The following writing and sharing tools will help eliminate untruths and negative mind chatter, as well as the feelings that can bring you down. My very specific writing technique disolve half or more of sad, mad or creepy feelings of rejection, many times your hurt or anger will vanish in thin air after writing. And you can breathe.

Never Fear! Writing and Tools are Here

Sometimes just thinking of having a feeling can be scary. I used to think if I cried and became sad or got mad, the feeling would not go away! I was wrong. I was afraid that facing the feeling would take me down. But actually, it does just the opposite! I was told as a teen, "Mimmy they are just feelings." OK . . . great. So, now what? I didn't have the *action tools* to deal with them. My feelings wanted to be recognized. I didn't know how to do this. But you will. Yes, your feelings *just want to be recognized.* They are like little babies. You stick a bottle in their mouths. Work with them using one or more of the tools (sharing, Pivoting, Mind Police, writing) and they'll quiet down. Soon enough, you'll let them go. Cry, scream, cry some more, write, and maybe share with a trusted friend. Pick your favorite tool! The deepest and most effective tool is writing what you feel. And if tears come . . . all the better.

Cry, scream, cry some more, write, and maybe share with a trusted friend. Pick your favorite tool! The deepest and most effective tool is writing what you feel. And if tears come . . . all the better.

CLUELESS IN TEXAS

How many feelings can you list? Many years ago, a very wise lady asked me to list my feelings. I remember that very day. I could only list three! Happy, mad, and sad. I am embarrassed to say I was well out of my twenties. Does this mean I went through high school and college not knowing how to identify my feelings? Sometimes I did not. And sometimes I gave my feelings way too much power. I did not know I could identify the feeling, sit and write about it and then redirect my mind. But I thank God I did know my boundaries and values. This alone got me to recognize and redirect my thoughts and actions. Keeping healthy boundaries saved me until I learned about *feeling management*.

Having boundaries is a self-esteem saver over and over again, especially where sexual activity is concerned. Self-restraint and delayed gratification will not always be your first choice, but you will be glad for the rest of your life that you started a *conscious boundary practice* during adolescence, especially when you are not clear on your feelings. This will not only safeguard your heart, but your body and you will enter college and/or your adult work years with little regret.

> You will be glad for the rest of your life that you started a conscious boundary practice during adolescence, especially when you are not clear on your feelings. This will not only safeguard your heart, but your body

Example: *Let's say a situation, or person, leaves you with an unsure feeling or a feeling that you are less than or unworthy.* No matter what occurred, first identify what the yucky feeling is. When you are back home by yourself, stop and check in with the feeling. Are you still feeling it a little or a lot? You may quickly find it not to be much of anything. But if you are still confused, hurting, frustrated or mad, it's worth taking the time to write about. This is actually an act of self-love. Why? Your feelings are connected to your heart and Spirit. And please just remember... to not judge your feeling as good or bad.

238

JOURNAL TIME

CREATE A LIST OF FEELINGS

1. Write down every feeling you can think of.
   If you can find 5 you are doing good. 10 even better.
   20-Wow!
2. List the feelings you believe you feel the most often.
3. List the feelings you would like to feel more often.

There is a list of feelings at the end of the book, but please try not to look, *yet*. It will amaze you how many there are. The more you know, the better you come to know you. And you are what is most important.

WRITING

Writing out your feelings is a type of magic.
Writing is an act of self-love.

INSIGHT & CLARITY

Writing, identifying a feeling and crying, are the deepest and most effective ways to deal with feelings. Writing is a great way to get ahold of bad feelings and false beliefs and shine an honest light on them. Writing out feelings is a practice, and an act of self-love. It will lift you up and out of whatever you may be telling yourself. Just because Jason (or whatever his name was) didn't say or do what you believed was right doesn't make you the victim, unless you let it fester and grow, and get hairy like that sandwich you left in your locker for three weeks. Clear it out with writing!

Writing is a sacred practice that allows you to get to your heart. This in turn allows you to know a deep and pure love for yourself that no one can take away! It's natural and human to play mental and emotional mind games. But ending the mind game happens through writing and exposing the lies you have been telling yourself. Over time, this allows you to deeply honor the real you, forever and ever. **Should you choose** to share your writing—please do so only with someone you believe is trustworthy, will not judge you and honors you as a person. This does not necessarily mean a friend. With or without sharing your writing, the next day truly becomes a new one! And carrying that hurt or angry feeling you've stuffed in the back of your underwear drawer? Poof! It is no longer an option.

> Writing is a sacred practice that allows you to get to your heart. This in turn allows you to know a deep and pure love for yourself that no one can take away!

You will oftentimes see the thought or feeling you believed to be so real, dissolve after identifying the feeling.

THE BEST WORK YOU'LL EVER DO

A Specific Writing Tool That Changed My Life.

JOURNAL TIME

FEELINGS

Let's start with the fun stuff to get you used to identifying your feelings. Please use the feeling list you created a few pages back. A list of feelings is also on the last page of this chapter.

Examples:

> I love the way I dress when I don't have to care about what anyone thinks. It makes me feel _____.

> When I run into the ocean and feel the water it makes me feel _____. (wet doesn't count!)

> When I hand a homeless person a dollar bill it makes me feel _____.

Let's step it up. You can't do it wrong.

Practice 1

Pick a feeling for each of these and write it down.

A. When I walk past a girl in a wheelchair and I can see her disabilities, if I don't acknowledge her by saying Hi or look her eyes and smile, it makes me feel _____.

B. When I overhear two girls gossiping about another girl I know, it makes me feel _____.

C. I was with a group of boys and they started slamming a girl I know and saying she was a ho or "loose," or some such, and it made me feel _____.

> NOTE: Writing "I'm glad I'm not her" doesn't count—it's not an *identified* feeling.

D. I met Chrissy at the locker three days ago. She told me what Robby said about not thinking I was his type, and it made me feel _____.

TWO JEWELS - Going Deeper

Sometimes, the *first feeling* is *not* the deeper feeling. Time to go deeper. THIS IS SAFE. This will help you know

A. How you really feel

B. That these feelings do not have control over you.

Knowing the above is key to personal power. It is *just a feeling.* And some feelings change or go away when the light is shown on them. How freeing to know.

Let's continue: You will sometimes need to write <u>two or three feelings</u> to discover the real one.

PRACTICE 2

Think of something that made you really hurt or mad.
1. Write down briefly the situation.
2. Now write the first feeling that happened.

Example 1 (on anger)

"I was feeling <u>pissed off.</u>" (anger). Now, keep going . . . "and that makes me *feel* _____ " (mad), and that makes me feel._____ . . (I hate her) and that makes me *feel* like _____(several descriptive words) "

This deeper identifying opens your heart, calms it down (and you may well cry... this is good and very good) which **allows the feeling to pass.** Yippee!!
- **Example 2 (being hurt)**

"Seeing Robbie at his locker made me feel angry. Because I know I am much cooler than he has a clue about. And this makes me feel _____*and that makes me feel* _____ *(frustrated, hurt, deeply sad, rejected, abandoned . . .) and that makes me really feel* _____*."*(write it out)

PRACTICE 3

Now, write in your journal about a real situation that made you feel mad or hurt. Or both!
NOTE: As you first start to write, you might be just blaming and accusing everybody (to get out the frustration). This is OK at first. But, challenge yourself to go deeper (you can do this), and really identify your feelings. When you do this, *you will come to know in your heart* whether you are being honest in your writing. You will begin to feel weirdly confident. Somehow you know that you're on your way to becoming a more grounded and happier person.

1-2 paragraphs are good.
Please give yourself permission (big word here . . . PERMISSION) to *feel the feelings* and then do the work.

You may find yourself saying, *"What the @#$$&!! I didn't know I felt rejected,".* This is what you could discover. As soon as you find the *feeling* word you have faced it . . . then BINGO! It loses half if not all its power. Remember, it's just a *feeling.* And feelings pass. ☺

> Please give yourself permission (big word here . . . PERMISSION) to feel the feelings and then do the work.

The magic of writing is finding the real feeling as you write it.

This may seem too simple a way to deal with very intense feelings. It is simple, but it is not always easy. And it's not for sissies. *I dare you.* You may find yourself crying at times as you write. *This is good, and very good.* Think of the situation and write about how it made you feel. Now say to your feelings, "Thank you for sharing. You may now leave." The lie, the fear, the craziness may go away completely.

YOUR BIGGEST JOB

Your biggest job is not school. It is the practice of recognizing your feelings and taking the action to put them in perspective. This is what also keeps you connected to your precious heart and Spirit. Writing, crying, letting go of it all and not blaming others is key. Why? Well for starters, you don't want to take it out on them. But, also, most people never change. But, you can change your attitude and keep from fooling yourself and others simply by writing out your feelings. And no, you will not die if dorkface doesn't ask you out or doesn't like you! It's OK to cry about it for a minute or two! Then it's . . . NEXT!

Add note: I must share this wonderful truth about crying. Let's say you are writing about

> Your biggest job is not school. It is the practice of recognizing your feelings and taking the action to put them in perspective. This is what also keeps you connected to your precious heart and Spirit.

your feelings. Something very sad comes up. Allowing yourself to cry is so important. Never feel bad about crying. And here is why: I once heard "Our tears touch the soul of God." I know this to be true. Crying happens when we are able to feel our own deep Spirit. Allow yourself this intimate personal response. knowing you are loved . . . no matter what... no matter what!

> Crying happens when we are able to feel our own deep Spirit. Allow yourself this intimate personal response.⁻ knowing you are loved . . . no matter what... no matter what!

Our tears touch the soul of God

*You can always grow yourself
to be the best of
who you were created to be. Allow no one to
tell you otherwise.*

C H A P T E R   1 5

LOVING YOURSELF

Three tools -Three Gifts-Only You Can Give Yourself

Before you graduate from the school of <u>Love and Life in the 21st Century,</u> ☺ there are a few more tools and gifts to give you. Then you may go back out in to this big world of ours with more knowledge, cool Life Skill tools, and the confidence to do what your heart and Spirit pull you towards.

3 TOOLS

Though a bit dramatic I can see you doing this first one in front of a friend or two.

Tool 1: PIVOTING – The Hand & Mind Police

Check in with you. What is going on right now? What do you feel at the end of this school day? Tired, relieved, overwhelmed, teased, or terrific? Check in with the feeling. I cannot stress enough how important it is to ask yourself. "How am I feeling right now? It is a good habit and a way to be *kind* to yourself. If you are feeling mad or less than, and there is no time to write, pivoting is great.

Most negative thinking are simply bad habits. Stopping a feeling or thought, *right in its tracks*, is where pivoting can help. The habit of saying to yourself things like *I'm such an idiot, School is too hard for me*, or *Those girls hate me because...*(fill in the blank) can sometimes be a "mind lie." Either way, to this, say "PIVOT!" Put your arm straight out and flip your hand outward. Maybe even step out your leg—bend it like in Warrior Pose and yell, "No, no, no! That's a lie!" Congratulations, you've just made a decision to shut off the negative self-talk or feeling-bad habit.

It is your right and responsibility to tell your mind to hush up sometimes. In truth, it is another act of act of self-love.Take that thing(a bad scene or nasty comment) your mind can't seem to get free of. Say to yourself, "NO-NO-NO. THAT'S A LIE!" Put your hand out like a great Police detective. Tell your mind to take a nice hike off a cliff. The Mind Police are the best police. You're the captain. Hurts and disappointments will happen; it's part of living real life. We make it worse, with our exaggerated beliefs and feelings:beliefs and feelings that are often not even true! You may have slipped unconsciously and decided to play a drama queen.

People may do head-trips on you. That's hippie talk. Think Lucky Brand –the apparel store ☺. But if you take it in... woah... let the false thinking begin! No. No. You must tell the not-so-smart mind, **"No. No. No. That's a lie!"**

If you love playacting, you can do this in front of a mirror. Just catch yourself bad-talking

It is your right and responsibility to tell your mind to hush up sometimes. In truth, this is an act of self-love. Take that thing (a bad scene or nasty comment) your mind can't seem to get free of. Say to yourself, "NO, NO, NO. THAT'S A LIE!"

yourself silently or aloud. The simple Hand & No routine works wonders on your self-esteem.

Self-esteem increases tenfold the day you decide not to trash yourself with 'little me' mind thoughts.

Did you know that many kids in Third World countries, because of limited to zero media, think they are lovable just because they exist? They simply feel it deep down. Guess they didn't see *Mean Girls* and then experience it in real life, at least like we do in developed countries. Keep in mind that school, friends, parents, and guys, and social yappity-yap—all that may *seem* important, but they are a small part of this thing called "Life," and it does change.

Simply choose to believe you are a loving creation. Because you are.

Tool 2: ACT AS IF—A Great Life Skill

As weird as it sounds, just act as if . . . sometimes even when you are unsure of everything! The day will come when you really do know a lot. Wow, and to think so many adults still do not!

The Act-As-If tool can be a life saver and a great technique when in a tight or confusing situation. I used to think it meant I was acting fake/not real. I did not like it when I first heard about it. Miss Honesty (me) needed to chill out and not be so honest and upfront at certain times. So . . . I tried it. I am a a big believer in telling the truth, the truth is most people are going to do and say what they want. Causing a scene with my own truth-sharing is not always helpful. Get what I mean?

Example:
There's a hassle between two friends you are with at the mall. One friend starts overreacting. Ask yourself, *Is this their stuff or mine?* Now, remind yourself, *I don't need to concern myself with the drama. It's not taking*

> Though I am a big believer in telling the truth, the truth is most people are going to do and say what they want. Causing a scene with my own truth-sharing is not always helpful.

anything of real value away from me. Simply *Act as if* they will soon get over what ever has them freaking out. Just smile with lips closed and . . . *voilà!* Allow them to take ownership of the whole thing.

Tool 3: LOVING DETATCHMENT

Example:
Two of your friends are arguing about the same boy. You are the bystander. Hey, listen if you care to. But as you see them start to really get into it ask yourself, *How important is this to me?* You can care about your friends without having to take sides. Mentally say to yourself, *I am choosing to detach from this situation.* **There's a saying I love to think quietly, or say aloud:**

"Not my circus. Not my monkey!" Voila! You're at peace.

As a teen, you may think you have little power, but recognizing that a scene or drama setup may happen and directing your mind to "detach" is a scene-preventer and friendship saver. Loving detachment or just friggin detaching from something that is not yours is an emotional *heart tool* to keep for life.

These three tools alone can move you on your way to becoming a much wiser human being than the past two generations, and in a much shorter time. You now have 3 usable Life Skill tools most people never receive. Unlike past generations, do not wait till midlife to find out how to use them. Even as a teen you'll be able to respond (instead of reacting) in a cool and sane way many adults have yet to learn.

> Directing your mind to "detach" is a scene-preventer and friendship save. Loving detachment or just friggin detaching from something that is not yours.

A Word of Warning

None of these tools work without your conscious help. They happen because you made a decision at the time- to *honor your heart, listen to your Spirit, and use your intuition* in a situation. However, if you are disconnected to that place deep inside you . . . (that means high, drunk/stoned, or unconscious from other zone-out practices) these gifts and tools are probably a pipe dream. Get the picture? Let's continue.

GIFT 1: Time - The Gift That Keeps on Giving

When you take the time to really know yourself, you'll find it easier to get know a guy you think is special. Learning about his personality—and what makes him tick—happens as you both practice real communication, i.e. on the phone at night (after homework, of course), and talking one-on-one in person. Yes, flirting and experiencing romance can happen when you are tuned in to *you*. Time allows the guy time to do the same (they often need more). And yes, timing and waiting are everything! Another basic no one really shares honestly with you about. **Your ability to take the time to communicate** with someone your thoughts with your voice, develops true caring. You will sense a feeling of being worthy. *With time* a boy often experiences *genuine* caring—not the premature "I really care about you" fueled purely by his hormones. He will be more attentive and thoughtful of you when he is allowed to give and receive the gift/experience of *real* communication.

> When you take the time to really know yourself, you'll find it easier to get know a guy you think is special. Learning about his personality—and what makes him tick—happens as you both practice real communication, i.e. on the phone at night (after homework, of course), and talking one-on-one in person.

It is up to you to find ways to value yourself and your body. Time out to practice yoga stretching calms the mind and centers the heart. The gift here will surprise you. One day you will notice yourself feeling of value...not just of your body but your mind, your heart, you're very being. Yoga stretch is a simple practice you can't do wrong. And you can do it in your bedroom.

> It is up to you to find ways to value yourself and your body. Time out to practicing yoga stretching calms the mind and centers the heart. The gift here will surprise you.

Concerning physically intimate encounters? Well, to be blunt, (What? Me blunt?) to engage in a physical sex act for a boy's physical release and for you as an experiment is a NAO (not an option). If a boy is unwilling to take the time to get to know you, so be it. But please remember . . . *never chase him.* It's a Boundary and Standard thing. This is a Golden Rule; if you follow it, you will deeply increase your self-worth.

Taking your time minimizes unneeded heartbreak and grows your self-esteem. Only you can give yourself this gift. Going slow is a gift to you and any boy lucky enough to take the time to know you. This is a precious time in your life. You must give yourself permission to take lots and lots of time.

> If a boy is unwilling to take the time to get to know you, so be it. But please remember . . . never chase him. It's a Boundary and Standard thing. This is a Golden Rule; if you follow it, you will deeply increase your self-worth.

GIFT TWO: Knowing Your Heart and Spirit Are Connected to Your Sexuality

> Your sexuality, all through life, will always be connected to your Spirit, the deepest part of you. Most girls today flat out don't know this. And it is the main reason girls feel used, yucky, and thrown away after a sexual act.

Your sexuality, all through life, will always be connected to your Spirit, the deepest part of you. Most girls today flat out don't know this. And it is the main reason girls feel used, yucky, and thrown away after a sexual act. Since the Sexual Revolution, many women have tried to act like men—but still acknowledge their value. The last 20 years that has changed.

Grown women too want to do what they want (their sex drive) and often block their deepest feelings. Believe it or not, our sexual desires are not our deepest feelings. **The second gift** allows you to *own a sense of you being worthy* and that you are strong. This inner knowing (like a whisper it is) can assist you in building your self-esteem. You don't have to do three perfect flips and be a cheerleader. Or even dress, weigh, or act a certain way. You do have to be *conscious* and in charge of your own body. Your heart and unique Spirit are gifts that keep on giving- so respect them.

The real world needs girls who understand and respect the heart and Spirit connection. Why? Because this relationship, when honored, helps you slowly but surely develop a keen sense of who you are and what you deserve.

> The real world needs girls who understand and respect the heart and Spirit connection.

GIFT THREE: Listen Breathe Allow -A simple meditation technique

Listen Breathe Allow is a **meditation** technique for the highly creative soul, for the A D D soul (Attention Deluxe & Divine), the ADHD (Attention Deluxe & Heavenly Divine) soul, or any girl that just wants to know *peace* within herself
Instructions: (ya can't do this wrong)

a. *Go somewhere quiet. Absolute quiet is not required . . . but minor sounds, or no noise, is best.*

b. *Sit comfortably and begin to breathe in slowly and out slowly*

1. **Close your eyes** and keep breathing.

2. While being still, **start to identify silently**, in your mind, all you are hearing.

Example: *Say to yourself silently- on the exhale, "I* hear my breathing"

    a. I hear the hum of the . . . dishwasher, refrigerator . . .
    b. I hear the traffic . . .
    c. I hear kids playing outside . . .
    d. I hear my family talking . . .
    e. I hear the wind outside my window, etc.

If wind is blowing on you (from outside or a fan), maybe think -*"I feel the fan," or "I hear the fan."*

2. If there is no sound (which I often experience), I will often say silently

    "I hear the *silent ringing"* -as there is often a ringing somewhere . . . likely its internal.
Side note: a yoga guru loved that one! ☺

3. **NOW,** *after you run out of things* to hear or notice.
4. *- just count your breath. Count silently on the exhale.* At around the count of 15 to 30 breaths you will be tired of counting. Your mind by now, has really slowed down—which is the goal . . . YIPPEE! Just chill as this slow down can take awhile.
5. **NOW –** A L L O W yourself to do nothing. *Simply allow your thoughts to float* in and out. . . . . . gently allow them to pass. You may or may not get a glimpse of *total*
stillness. And that's totally cool. Even if your mind does not go to those few seconds of total silence

Your meditation is successful! Why? Because it is healing brain cells just by practicing meditation. How cool is that? You have taken the time and allowed your brain to de – stress. This is success!

Twenty minutes is the standard. Fifteen is good. If you can do ten, start there. It can easily take 9 to 11 minutes to experience a chilled mind. Everyone is different and most important—<u>you cannot do this wrong.</u>

YOU ARE SPECIAL, NATURALLY

I hope you are starting to see that our world needs all girls to love themselves more than the attention they may or may not receive from a guy. Young women who have taken the time to develop communication and self-esteem can move mountains.

In the United States, women are 51 percent of the population, but only 17 percent of women are in Congress. Only thirty-four have been governors. Sixty-seven countries have had female presidents or prime ministers. *But not the United States.* This dominant male thing is not helping us prevent wars. Men often lack the perception and insight needed for big decision making. It's time your country hears from you. ☺ Kind of like Emma Gonzalez.

THINKING BIGGER

What might it take for you to think, feel and then believe, "I am a leader?" In the early '70s women fought hard for basic rights in the work force,

What might it take for you to think, feel and then believe, "I am a leader?" In the early '70s women fought hard for basic rights in the work force, for reproductive rights and equal pay.

256

for reproductive rights and equal pay. The last couple of generations have taken the above for granted. And as I write this today we are finding great upheaval in all human norms and standards. You are here *now* for a reason ---and you have knowledge the last two generations did not receive.

I hope **YBG** has given you enough hidden info and shared enough to motivate you to practice conscious behavior and love for yourself. primarily. Only then can we help break the valueless, unconscious behavior of humanity and make life better on this planet.

You are that important.

Why do you think so many girls are allowing themselves to be used and abused today? Let's make a pact. If a girlfriend you care about is sliding towards acting and talking like a soon-to-be Hodomville High graduate, slip her a love note. Remind her she is loved and on this amazing planet for a reason. Tell her that her heart and Spirit can rock this world and it needs her. Neither of you need to know what the reason is. That's what life journeys are for. But it's a fact you will own and be proud of one day.

I recently heard that Spirit has hope all through It. Hope is a form of faith. It would be so cool if more girls started thinking higher and honoring their selves with class and style- (just a little is cool) and can be done with very little money. caring, and owning *the fact that* . . .

We are here to make a difference.

Armed with Life Skill tools and the bigger picture, and knowing the importance of your heart, body, mind, and Spirit, you now have what it takes to carry yourself with grace and potential through this life here on earth. One thing is for sure: what we do is always a choice, always. Good travels. And never forget this fact:

You are whole and loved and perfect.
You were born that way...
No matter what. No matter what.

Sure, adolescence is a tricky time—but, so is young adulthood and all the other stages in life! You now have some basic life skill tools, tools many adults don't ever find unless they hit a bottom emotionally in midlife and seek help. You will enter your twenties, equipped with, not only a self-esteem saver but a wonderful pathway to loving yourself for life . . . no matter what.

I thank you mucho for being open and willing to read this book to the very end. Please continue working in your journal. I promise it will help you live your **one big beautiful life** fully here on planet earth - *less stressed* - knowing there really are *no big deals*. Yippee!

With love and excitement in all you are becoming,

Your Great Aunt Mimmy ☺

THE FEELINGS LIST

Sad	loved
Frightened	appreciated
Hurt	crushed
Tense	Proud
Frustrated	excited
Anxious	content
Insecure	warm
Less than	relaxed
Confused	calm
Bored	comfortable
Weak	strong
Shocked	flat
Pressured	surprised
Uncomfortable	over the top
Annoyed	confident
Furious	loved
purposeful	Hurt
Happy	grateful

Pleased	sexy
Glad	determined
Wonderful	forgiving
Elated	hopeful
motivated	mad
fantastic	threatened
strong	worthless
vivacious	less than
vivid	capable
caring	smart
cool	rejected
inspired	abandoned
bitter	paranoid
flat	eager
useless	receptive
empty	FEEL Free to add others!

LOVE-OUT OF THIS WORLD-
MUSIC LIST

GREAT SOFT LOVE & LOVE ROCK MUSIC

Feel the Love- this love is inside YOU! Yes.
Even without a boyfriend. Yep. It is so cool. These
human feelings of passion and fun can happen lots
of times. You wanna see your parents act weird?
Just watch them as they listen to some of thes tunes.

SO WHY WOULD I GIVE YOU A LIST OF
SONGS that you have probably never heard?
Becuase these are songs tht create feelings of love
& Joy and stay in your heart forever.
**DO A SLUMBER PARTY & YOUTUBE SOME OF THESE.
LISTEN TO THE WORDS.** Better yet.- Listen alone - in
the privacy of your bedroom.
OLDIE GOLDIES CAN ROCK YOUR WORLD

1. Feel love...and dance love! Yes,feel what love feels like.
2. Now DANCE! Practice dance moves that don't simulate
   sex. Just move your arms and hips in a way that is sensual
   (sideways) not pornified.
Hey, do you really want to dance in a prom dress or a pair of
jeans simulating porn moves? Peleeeeeease!

I will start with the oldest CLASSICS... some you may
recognize.
ENJOY THESE...NO GUY REQUIRED!

SUPER GOLDEN OLDIES- LOVE SONGS
Super fun to act out... and filled with LOVE.
SHA- LA- LA MUSIC OF THE MID 60s... total love
based and fun to sing along with.
Slumber party music. Sweet & innocent

THE SHIRELLES - *THE First All girl band in
Teen Rock History to be NO. 1 on the charts.

If you are a singer, musician or lover of music...
THIS LIST will OPEN UP & rock your world.

YOUTUBE ALL OF THESE

Baby It's You * (THE ULTIMATE Sha la la song)**
Soldier Boy
Dedicated to the One I Love
Tonight's the Night *
Will You Still Love Me Tomorrow *

Remakes by
Linda Ronstadt. Carol King, Amy Winehouse
Great One HIT Wonders
Be My Baby *   The Ronettes
Baby I'm Yours***   Barbara Lewis
Just One Look *   Doris Troy –

NAME OF SONG	THE BAND
Brown Eyed Girl	Van Morrison
These Eyes ***	The Guess Who
It's Too Late Baby	Carol King
Whiter Shade of Pale	Procol Harem
Sunshine of Your Love	Cream
Helplessly Hoping	Crosby, Stills & Nash Peter
Glory of Love	Cetera
Happy Man ***	**Chicago** (hard to find but SO
September	LOVE FILLED)
Please Please Me	The Beatles

DRIPPY SWEET LOVEY DOVEY ☺

We've Only Just Begun	The Carpenters
Cherish Is The Word	**The Association** **
I Wanna Make It With You *	**Bread** **
Just My Imagination	The Temptations
Just Once In My Life ***	**The Righteous Bros.**
You've Lost That Loving Feeling	
You Are Not Alone	Michael Jackson
Dream Dream Dream	Everly Bros.
Up on The Roof	**The Drifters**
In My Room	**The Beach Boys**

FUN DANCE IT OUT MUSIC

ANY thing in BOLD are MY FAVORITES - the first by Mariah is the bomb.

Dream Lover *	Mariah Carey
	(totally fun to dance to)
Wa Watussi	(too funny! The YT video)
The Loco-motion (funny, cute)	**Kylie Minogue.version**
Love Shack	B-52s

TIMELESS ENGLISH & U S LOVE ROCK

Under My Thumb	**The Rolling Stones**
Let It Whip	Dazz Band
Dazz	Brick
Tell It to Me Slowly*	**The Zombies**
She's Not There	
Time of the Season	
You Really Got Me	**The Kinks**
Louie Louie	
All The Day & All..	
It's My Life	The Animals
Soul Kitchen	**The Doors**
Back Door Man	
Hello I Love You	
Roadhouse Blues	
L A Woman	
Black Magic Woman	Santana
Can't Find My Way Home	Blind Faith
Sunshine of Your Love	Cream

Great Rock Love songs by Led Zeppin - see last page

SEXY LOVEY SLOWLY

No Ordinary Love ***	Sade
By Your Side **	
Smooth Operator **	
Killing Me Softly ***	**Roberta Flack**
Wrong Side of Town	Johnny Rivers
Tracks of My Tears	
My Girl	The Temptations

265

Hello It's Me
Daisy Jane

Tod Rudgren
America

Ever Green *
The Way We Were
Walk on By ***
(Whitney Houston's aunt)
California ***

Barbra Streisand

Dione Warwick (cry city)

**Joni Mitchell (hippie chick
of the world)**

Love Me Tender
Are You Lonesome Tonight
Blue Hawaii

Elvis Presley

Your Are Everything
Let's Stay Together

The Stylistics
Al Green

Heart Full of Soul
For Your Love

The Yard Birds

Whole Lotta Love
Stairway To Heaven
Heart Breaker

Led Zepplin

Its All In The Name of Love
I'm So Lonsome...
Lady Of The Canyon
Long Way From China

Jimmie Spheeris

A C K N O W L E D G E M E N T S

Each tell a story

My two grown sons who walked through the Clinton fiasco in Middle School, sharing honest comments & reflections from a summer camp incident, tolerating me loading you and your buddies up for Sex Ed. workshops at the downtown Presbyterian Church.

The Agoura Hills Public Library and staff. What a beautiful office it offered me.

Michael Herman my male angel in New York- a phone call away with emotional and tech support, no matter what.

Ben Swilhart my last hired content editor. His patience with such a project is deeply appreciated.

My 6 nieces in Texas -Kaylee, Bethany, Mary Hollon, Katherine, Callie, Cameron & Mary Kristen

Michael Beckwith, his book **Life Visions** and his *bigger than life* encouraging words at **Agape** over the years sharing repeatedly until it stuck –'We must do what has *never been done before.*'

Rickie Byers for her many musical inspirations blasting through my car speakers day after day, year after year.

All the mothers who voiced their concerns over the years on this over whelming subject

Marie Wilson, mother, Girl Scout Leader, and actor. Who ..when I mentioned I was *considering* doing **YBG** shared- *oh, yes. Please, please do one. My daughter is only 10 but we need one.* The sincerity in her voice was my first wake- up call.

My first editor - 14-year-old girl from Newbury Park- after reading a sit com scene wrote-*They stole our innocence* in red pen.

Ann Redus who is pure spirit, part angel, and dear friend.

Ginger Green who- as President of Planned Parenthood in Amarillo, Texas asked me to be on the board.
Claudia Blackburn- Head of the Dept. of Health and co-founder of High plains Pregnancy Coalition

The mother I met at the **Calabasas Commons** who shared frantically of Kylie Jenner walking by her eighth grader who started crying- saying, '*Oh, she's my idol.*'

The many editors who wanted to religio-size,, academic-ize or change the voice... **and I refused.**

Carmen-My millinial roommate's kindness and chill factor

Dee Gee from Peru -A beautiful 21 year old who sat for hours with me when I asked "Does this sound ok?"

The 24 year- old wholesale girl at **Magic** in 2015 who shared -*I feel so bad about what I was doing at 14 and 15. Please get it out there,* **The 27-year-old** female who shared at age 12 her addiction to erotic literature on her flip phone. **Houston, Texas Freshman**- who shared a telling flip comment When asked - *why would a fifteen-year-old girl ...*

Beverly Bishop – an etiquette instructor who helped me with **The 5 Biggees.**

Dr. David Chastain – who helped deliver my two 10 pounders and shared current information

The many techies who shared on the phone personal stories and their concern and sadness at what their younger siblings and step siblings are exposed to.

All the males ages 15 to 50 who shared how they are dealing with sexuality, what they like and do not like- and their willingness to share concerns about females coming on to them & not finding the right kind of girl.

Megan Reilly -young author who reflected honestly about **YBG** in its final edit.

The professional women in the educational field and university level who were *willing* to share.

Adina Nack sociology professor and expert in sexuality.

The CDC – and our Government for supporting it. **The Ventura County** Aids Awareness organizers.

All my library buddies who shared candy, print paper, comments beautiful smiles for 6 plus years. Dennis, Rowe, and many others.

To every musician & singer in the 60s & 70s who knew how to rock a love song, sweeten a love ballad, and create great music lyrics that stand today as *love poetry.* Life is so happy on days I play your songs decades later. I am still overwhelmed with gratitude. Thank you.

To every guy I ever kissed and enjoyed it! ☺

It takes what it takes. ☺

BREATHE!

Made in the USA
San Bernardino, CA
28 May 2019